NICHOLAS OF CUSA AND THE KAIROS OF MODERNITY

CASSIRER, GADAMER, BLUMENBERG

Nicholas of Cusa and the Kairos of Modernity

Cassirer, Gadamer, Blumenberg

Michael Edward Moore

dead letter office

BABEL Working Group

punctum books ∗ brooklyn, ny

NICHOLAS OF CUSA AND THE KAIROS OF MODERNITY:
CASSIRER, GADAMER, BLUMENBERG
© Michael Edward Moore, 2013.

First published in 2013 by
dead letter office, BABEL Working Group
an imprint of punctum books
Brooklyn, New York
http://punctumbooks.com

The **BABEL Working Group** is a collective and
desiring-assemblage of scholar-gypsies with no lead-
ers or followers, no top and no bottom, and only a
middle. BABEL roams and stalks the ruins of the
post-historical university as a pack, looking for other
roaming packs with which to cohabit and build
temporary shelters for intellectual vagabonds. We
also take in strays.

ISBN-13: 978-0615840550
ISBN-10: 0615840558

Cover Image: Hans Kruse, "Morning on Karls Bridge,"
Prague, Czech Republic (2006); reprinted with per-
mission of photographer.

Editorial-Creative Team: Brianne Harris, Eileen Joy,
and Kate Workman

TABLE OF CONTENTS

PREFATORY NOTE

𝄞

I am grateful to Daniel O'Connell and my colleague Jennifer Sessions for their careful reading and scholarly assistance with this essay; and to Günther Hönicke who helped me to visit the chapel and library of Nicholas of Cusa and whose garden was a placid setting in which to study. Following my lecture on this topic at the Medieval Congress in Kalamazoo, in 2013, comments and suggestions were graciously offered by members of the American Cusanus Society: many thanks to Donald Duclow, Thomas Izbicki, Peter Casarella, and Mirela Oliva. My research was further assisted by librarians at the Leo Baeck Institute in Manhattan. For Eileen Joy: "Autumn already! — But why regret the everlasting sun, if we are sworn to a search for divine brightness?" (Rimbaud, "Adieu").

Iowa City, 20 February 2013

Viele täuschet Anfang / Und Ende

Beginning and end
Greatly deceive us

~Friedrich Hölderlin[*]

In omnibus faciebus videtur facies
facierum velate et in aenigmate.

In all faces the Face of Faces is seen,
veiled and enigmatically.

~Nicholas of Cusa[**]

---

[*] Friedrich Hölderlin, "At One Time I Questioned the Muse," in *Poems and Fragments*, trans. Michael Hamburger (London: Anvil Press Poetry, 2004), 635.
[**] Nicholas of Cusa, *Opera Omnia*, vol. VI, *De Visione Dei*, ed. Adelaida Dorothea Riemann (Hamburg: In Aedibus Felicis Meiner, 2000), 23; my translation [cited hereafter as: *De Visione*, ed. Riemann].

I. MODERNITY

A debate over the origins of European modernity unfolded among philosophers and historians in the century following the publication of Jacob Burckhardt's *Civilization of the Renaissance in Italy* (1860). The figure of Nicholas of Cusa (1401-1464) was an important part of these studies and discussions. While Cusanus escaped the notice of Burckhardt, he had a special importance for scholarship in the history of philosophy. In this context it was often debated whether Cusanus should be seen as the first modern thinker, or conversely, as the last great medieval mind. To question the modernity of Nicholas of Cusa was really a way to apprehend the meaning and shape of modernity. Whether Nicholas was assigned to the Middle Ages or to modern times would be the result of a basic interpretation of the character of modernity.

In Conrad Bursian's monumental history of philology in Germany, to choose one example, Cusanus fell to the medieval side of the line separating the Middle Ages from the Renaissance and Reformation. This was due to the fact that, in Bursian's view, although Nicholas was one of the first European scholars to engage in serious study of classical texts, he did so only for the purposes of theology and to serve the needs of the Church.[1] For the academic classicist Bursian, modernity meant secularization and freedom from the Church. Classical studies properly so-called were part of a new modern context for intellectual life. In Germany, the study of classical antiquity, *Alterthumswissenschaft*, was considered to be the very model of a modern university program. Classicism offered the means of defining modernity itself through its scientific grasp of earlier ages.[2]

The following essay explores the discussions regarding Cusanus and the origins of modernity that occurred among Ernst Cassirer, Hans-Georg Gadamer, and Hans Blumenberg. At the outset it should be said that these thinkers were all dedicated to a specific intellectual realm—to problems within the area of Europe-

---

[1] Conrad Bursian, Geschichte der classischen Philologie in Deutschland von den Anfängen bis zur Gegenwart (Munich: R. Oldenbourg, 1883), 90.

[2] Pierre Judet de la Combe, "Classical Philology and the Making of Modernity in Germany," in *Multiple Antiquities–Multiple Modernities. Ancient Histories in Nineteenth-Century European Cultures*, eds. Gábor Klaniczay, Michael Werner and Ottó Gecser (Frankfurt: Campus Verlag, 2011), 65 [65–88]. Another connection that will become important for our discussion is the influence of neo-Kantianism within the field of classical studies, as exemplified by J.G. Droysen.

an historical consciousness and the history of European ideas. As we shall see, modernity proved to be so complex an idea that the life and writings of Cusanus could scarcely correspond to it or be made to account for it. The point was not to turn Cusanus into a great founder of the modern world, but rather to identify within his writing the first symptoms of modernity. Out of the extensive corpus of Cusa's writings, here the *De Visione Dei* will serve as a focus. To understand the debate regarding the significance of Nicholas of Cusa for the origins of the modern world, we must take into account the existing historical literature on the Renaissance period, written in the late nineteenth and early twentieth centuries. Philosophy of that period was so thoroughly oriented toward historical problems and the history of ideas, that historical literature provides a crucial backdrop for understanding philosophical debates.

What is meant by the *emergence of modernity*? The meaning of the term is unfixed. The term *modern* can refer innocently enough to the present or the recent past, but also serves as a complex historical and literary term.[3] *Modernity* adds a further layer of significance, as an epoch having certain essential characteristics. The origin and significance of modernity became a major theme in early twentieth century literary criticism and philosophy. After Kant, it was asserted that philosophy could become modern by freeing itself from the confines of medieval Christian philosophy. Later (following Hegel)

---

[3] Cf. *Modernism, 1890-1930*, eds. Malcolm Bradbury and James McFarlane (Penguin: Harmondsworth, 1976).

thinkers of the late nineteenth and early twentieth centuries believed that philosophy must become ever more resolutely modern, if it hoped to account for modern experience in a world shaped by industrialization, technology and the new cosmos of modern science.[4] Modernity was therefore something new, specific to the time and place of industrialized Europe. How and when had it come into existence?

According to Friedrich Theodor Vischer, writing in 1846, modernity in literature emerged from the unrest of poets, painters and thinkers of the Renaissance who staged a "break with the Middle Ages."[5] For critics and philosophers alike, modernity was an unusually flexible concept, combining ideas about the course of European history with trends in literature and philosophy. Modernity is often said to have emerged as an intellectual break with the constraints and superstitions of the medieval past.

---

[4] According to Hegel, philosophy can teach resignation in the face of our alienation from cruel realities. The vast procedure of recollection and rethinking exposed in the *Phenomenology* is made possible by a twilight retrospective view of history. See Frederick Beiser, *Hegel* (New York: Routledge, 2005), 171. Löwith notes that in Hegel, history "finally achieves its full Being and knowing." Hegel saw himself as standing at the pinnacle of 2,500 years of history. See Karl Löwith, *Martin Heidegger and European Nihilism*, trans. Gary Steiner (New York: Columbia University Press, 1995), 198.

[5] "Bruch mit dem Mittelalter": F. T. Vischer, *Aesthetik oder Wissenschaft des Schönen*, cited in "Modern, die Moderne," in Joachim Ritter and Karlfried Gründer, *Historisches Wörterbuch der Philosophie* (Darmstadt: Wissenschaftliches Buchgesellschaft, 1984).

This dark *medieval* fog is pervasive in popular history-writing. For Stephen Greenblatt, for example, the Middle Ages was a time when education declined and commerce creaked to a halt: "schools closed, libraries and academies shut their doors" during "centuries of chaos" that followed the fall of Rome. As in a cowboy movie, "life was cheap."[6] Only the Renaissance discovery of antiquity was able to rescue the European mind from its medieval darkness. Modernity only becomes visible, one might think, when placed in front of a dark medieval curtain.[7] From their origins in the early nineteenth century, Renaissance studies were an inquiry into the origins of 'modern man.' The Renaissance was the first period of the "discovery of the world and the discovery of man," as Jules Michelet explained in his treatise of 1855, *Renaissance*.[8]

An examination of debates over the origins of modernity in the late-nineteenth and early twentieth centuries suggests that the term does

---

[6] Stephen Greenblatt, *The Swerve: How the World Became Modern* (New York: W.W. Norton, 2011), 24, 25, 38.

[7] Giuseppe Mazzotta, *The Worlds of Petrarch* (Durham: Duke University, 1993). Some aspects of the problem are addressed in Yossef Schwartz, "Ernst Cassirer on Nicholas of Cusa: Between Conjectural Know-ledge and Religious Pluralism," in Jeffrey Andrew Barash, *The Symbolic Construction of Reality: The Legacy of Ernst Cassirer* (Chicago: University of Chicago Press, 2008), 17–39.

[8] "Découverte du monde et découverte de l'homme": Jules Michelet, *Renaissance* (Paris: Chamerot, 1855), based on lectures given in 1840; cited in Salvatore Settis, *The Future of the "Classical"*, trans. Allan Cameron (Cambridge, Eng.: Polity Press, 2006), 53.

not clearly indicate a certain period of history (as a segment of time) but is really a messianic concept, taking its meaning from the horizon of a crisis (*kairos*), when an historical world-order passes through a painful moment of transformation.[9] Modernity is not only a decisive phase of history, but conceptually the arrival of a final phase, an end time of unknown duration. "Modernity is an ambiguous concept," suggests Judet de la Combe, because it has no fixed temporal boundary, and denotes "a period of time which is essentially open to the future because it is characterized as new, as provisory."[10] Furthermore, lying behind many interpretations of modern thought is the idea that modernity brought with it the possibility of understanding the truths of nature and humanity at last. Thus the poet Arthur Rimbaud's proclamation that "One must be absolutely modern" led him directly to the possibility that he might "be able now to possess the truth within one body and one soul."[11] Modernity would offer to humanity a *gnosis*, a special way of knowing standing above all earlier ways of knowing.

For early twentieth-century philosophy, modernity was the name for a kind of destiny. It implied a faith in progress not only in the sphere of thought and literature, but in regard

---

[9] Crisis, as used here, corresponds to the German theological term *Krise*, a central idea for Karl Barth and Paul Tillich.

[10] Judet de la Combe, "Classical Philology," 11.

[11] See discussion of Rimbaud's last work "Adieu" in Denis Hollier, *A New History of French Literature* (Cambridge, Mass.: Harvard University Press, 1989), 759–780.

to social goods from streetlights to impartial justice. In 1990 the philosopher Edgar Morin summarized the complex character of the idea of modernity, while locating its origins in the Renaissance: "Born at the end of the fifteenth century, modernity . . . was not just an historical phenomenon, nor only a dominant idea (*idée-force*), but a faith."[12] The complexity of the term, and the significance of modernity as a new stance in philosophy, explain why the concept should become a focus of philosophical concern in the first half of the twentieth century: philosophers began to debate the origins of modernity, as part of a more general effort to understand modernity and thus the situation of philosophy. As a mystic and philosopher during this momentous period of change, the writings of Nicholas of Cusa seemed to contain important clues about the coming of modernity.[13]

---

[12] Edgar Morin, *Le Monde*, February 14, 1990; cited in Jacques Boudet, *Les Mots de l'histoire* (Paris: Robert Laffont, 1990), 738–739.

[13] Themes in Cusa's philosophy that seem to have a 'modern' character are summarized in Jasper Hopkins, "Nicholas of Cusa (1401-1464): First Modern Philosopher?" *Midwest Studies in Philosophy* 16 (2002): 13–29.

II. Nicholas of Cusa

Modern philosophy would have to investigate its own history in order to understand its destiny. Thus it happened that, four hundred years after his death, the bold and idiosyncratic ideas of Nicholas of Cusa became the focal point for discussions among twentieth-century German philosophers about the origins of modernity, involving most prominently Ernst Cassirer (1847-1945), Hans-Georg Gadamer (1900-2002), and Hans Blumenberg (1920-1996). The debate was rooted in a shared conviction that philosophy and history were intertwined, in spite of the fact that these three thinkers belonged to contending branches of the German philosophical tradition.[14] Each thinker in his own way devel-

---

[14] The germ of the present essay was suggested by Mazzotta, *Worlds of Petrarch*, 15. The philosophical dispute between Martin Heidegger and Ernst Cassirer was the backdrop of these discussions. Indeed, both philosophers understood philosophy to be historically conditioned: see Peter Eli Gordon, *Continen-*

oped the "hermeneutics of thought as a historical phenomenon."[15] These philosophers saw the 'modernity of Nicholas of Cusa' as a problem in the history of European consciousness and the history of science and philosophy.

In the philosophical debate over modernity, Nicholas of Cusa unexpectedly took center stage. In spite of the impressive *corpus* of his writings, Cusanus was much less well-known, and much less popular, than other authors of the Renaissance period, such as Petrarch, Pico della Mirandola, or Erasmus. In spite of the careful publication of his collected works by the humanist Lefèvre d'Etaples in 1514, the writings of Cusanus had fallen like a stone into obscurity, until their gradual rediscovery in the late nineteenth century.[16] The fact that Nicholas was

---

tal *Divide: Heidegger, Cassirer, Davos* (Cambridge, Mass.: Harvard University Press, 2010), 10–11.

[15] Schwartz uses this expression of Cassirer in particular, but it is applicable to Gadamer and Blumenberg as well. See Schwartz, "Ernst Cassirer on Nicholas of Cusa," 26. This is the point at which Gadamer goes beyond Heidegger's understanding of the hermeneutical circle, by turning to historical study: which would later inspire the field of *Begriffsgeschichte.* The interpreter must learn "not to approach the text directly, relying solely on the fore-meaning already available to him, but rather explicitly to examine the legitimacy—i.e., the origin and validity—of the fore-meanings dwelling within him." As Gadamer explained, this calls for research into concepts and language of the past: Hans-Georg Gadamer, *Truth and Method,* 2d edn. (New York: Continuum, 1998), 267.

[16] *Haec Accurata Recognitio Trium Voluminum Operrum Clariss. P. Nicolai Cusae Card. Ex Officina As-*

such an obscure historical figure became part of the overall problem of 'Cusanus and modernity.' In the brief discussion of Nicholas of Cusa that follows I will focus on a single key work, the *De Visione Dei*, which featured prominently and significantly in the twentieth century debate. In this work, Cusanus presents a theory of how the manifold perspectives of individual human beings on God and the world can illuminate the infinite particular connections between God and human beings.

A gothic, enigmatic figure of the late Middle Ages, the personality and writings of Nicholas of Cusa seemed difficult and strange to succeeding ages, and so for a long time he was "veiled in a cloud of the past," in the phrase of the Carl Binz (1832-1913).[17] His writings did not circulate widely even during his lifetime. Flasch records the connection of Nicholas to scholarly Italian circles, but his writings were little quoted or mentioned.[18] The steady trickle of awareness and reception of his *opera* may nevertheless illustrate the paradoxical importance of little-known thinkers and the principle of

censiana Recenter Emissa Est, ed. Jacques Lèfevre d'Etaples (Josse Badius, 1514) [Wolfenbüttel: Herzog August Bibliothek, H: P 556.2° Helmst. (1)].

[17] "So hüllten die Nebel der Vergangenheit den Mann ein": Carl Binz, "Zur Charakteristik des Cusanus," *Archiv für Kulturgeschichte* 7 (1909): 145 [145–153]. Carl Binz (1832-1913) was a medical historian at the Bonn Institute of Pharmacology.

[18] Kurt Flasch, *Nikolaus von Kues. Geschichte einer Ent-wicklung. Vorlesunen zur Einführung in seine Philosophie* (Frankfurt-am-Main: Vittorio Klostermann, 1998), 219–225.

obscure influences at the heart of intellectual history.[19] The connections among Nicholas of Cusa and later thinkers such as Leonardo da Vinci (1452-1519), for example, are important, but the precise lines of influence are spidery and difficult to trace, even after the exhaustive researches of Pierre Duhem.[20] The humanism

---

[19] In this vein, the militant sociologist and philosopher Georges Friedmann believed that in order to transform the world, spiritual effort should be devoted not to crowds, but to small numbers of people, or even to single individuals. See Pierre Hadot, *What is Ancient Philosophy*, trans. Michael Chase (Cambridge, Mass.: Belknap Press, 2001), 280.

[20] Discussing a manuscript of Leonardo which exhibits many apparent signs of Cusanus' influence, Duhem issued a delicate network of negatives: "Il n'en est aucune où l'on ne puisse, sans effort, reconnaître une allusion à quelque partie de l'oeuvre de l'Évêque de Brixen": Pierre Duhem, "Nicolas de Cues et Léonard de Vinci," *Bulletin Italien* VII (1907): 87–134, 181–220, 314–329, and *Bulletin Italien* VIII (1908): 18–55, 116–147. This quotation: *Bulletin Italien* VII (1907): 181. The problem of *obscure influence* suggests that intellectual history, like art history, must take account of multiple frames of reference, and consider "cultural time" as a reference point, in addition to the unrolling of calendar years: see Erwin Panofsky, "Reflections on Historical Time," trans. Johanna Baumann, *Critical Inquiry* 30 (2004): 691–701. Compare with Hans Blumenberg, *The Legitimacy of the Modern Age*, trans. Robert M. Wallace (Cambridge, Mass.: MIT Press, 1983): "The fragment in codex 211 lay dormant until its rediscovery in the library of the hospice of Cusa; that would be the most external reason for the fact that it exercised no influence" (507). Kepler, however, called him "*Divinus mihi Cusanus*": cited in Edmond Vansteenberghe,

and science of Cusanus help explain his importance for later debates over the origins of modernity. On the other hand, in the post-metaphysical environment of twentieth-century German philosophy, the medieval framework of Cusa's thought, and his mysticism, seemed to distance him from the modern world.[21] Nicholas often described his own thought in mystical terms—describing the deepest level of theology to which he aspired as a meaningful darkness in which the mind, 'knowing without knowing,' voyaged beyond the edge of rational understanding (*intellectus*) in search of God—thereby entering a cloud (*caligo*).[22] Nicholas was fear-

---

Cardinal Nicolas du Cues (1401-1464): L'Action—la pensée (Paris: Honoré Champion, 1920), 450n3. Koyré flatly denied that Cusanus had any influence in the development of astronomy: see Alexandre Koyré, *The Astronomical Revolution, Copernicus—Kepler—Borelli*, trans. R.E.W. Maddison (Ithaca: Cornell University Press, 1973), 75; cited in Heiko A. Oberman, *The Dawn of the Reformation: Essays in Late Medieval and Early Reformation Thought* (Grand Rapids: Eerdmans Publishing, 1986), 182.

[21] In the analysis of Michel de Certeau, the *De Concordia Catholica* is modern in its individualism, and traditional in its "theological and mystical foundation": Michel de Certeau, "The Gaze: Nicholas of Cusa," *Diacritics* 17 (1987): 19 [2–38]. The view that modern thought could not also be theological or mystical can be found already in Émile Gebhart, *Les origines de la Renaissance en Italie* (Paris: Hachette, 1879), 323.

[22] Alois Maria Haas, *Deum mistice videre . . . in caligine coincidencie. Zum Verhältnis Nicolaus' von Kues zur Mystik*; Vorträge der Aeneas-Silvius-Stiftung an der Universität Basel, XXIV (Basel: Verlag Halbing & Lichtenhahn, 1989), 42.

less about emphasizing the difficulties of imagination that would confront his readers. It is as though he used this warning sign to prevent entry by anyone lacking in wakefulness or imagination.

Exceptionally learned, Cusanus wrote on a wide range of topics with flair and originality, assembling one of the largest private libraries of his day. This library certainly shows the connection between his interests and the greater cultural world of the Renaissance. It is still possible to visit the library, conserved in a room above the chapel in the St. Nikolaus Hospital, which he founded in his birthplace on the Mosel, Kues. The book cabinets contain a treasury of works by Aristotle, Thomas Aquinas and Ramón Lull, Pseudo-Dionysius, Roman and canon law, a collection of requisites for any medieval theologian or active churchman. Nicholas had copied some of these volumes himself, for his own use, in a lovely crisp humanistic hand. From an interior window of this library, one can look down to the floor of the chapel, where the heart of Nicholas lies buried under a brass tablet bearing his portrait. There on the floor before the altar, it is possible to place your hand over the heart of the portrait.[23] The question arises, whether these books and physical relics should be seen as the heart of modernity.

---

[23] While Nicholas's body was buried in Italy, his heart was returned to Kues and buried in front of the altar.

III. Nicholas of Cusa in the Renaissance

Cusanus was born in Bernkastel-Kues, to a prosperous family engaged in trading and shipping wine from the vineyards that rise steeply above the Mosel River. He completed his higher education in several universities: Heidelberg, then a center of conciliarist thought; Padua, where he studied law and was introduced to new trends in science and mathematics; and Cologne, where he studied theology and philosophy.[24] His writings, which are difficult to summarize, respond to a wide range of intellectual currents even beyond his university training: the *devotio moderna*, Christian neoplatonism, the inwardness of northern mystics such as Rulman Merswin and Meister Eckhart, and the genial bright-

---

[24] Morimichi Watanabe, *The Political Ideas of Nicholas of Cusa, with Special Reference to his* De Concordantia catholica (Geneva: Librairie Droz, 1963), 13–14.

ness of Italian humanism.[25]

Cusanus's mystically-tinged humanism is unusual because of his regard for the authenticity of individual human existence and physical actuality, as propounded in his work *De visione Dei.* In this work we come into contact with Cusa's distinctive *humanism of the other*, which was inspired by his humanistic fascination with ancient literature, but directed toward palpable living humanity and the particularity of actual human beings.[26] His understanding

[25] Still valuable is the older work of Vansteenberghe, *Le Cardinal Nicolas du Cues*, which should be compared however with more recent volumes (on Nicholas's education, see 6–16). A useful biographical sketch is provided by Donald F. Duclow, "Life and Works," in Christopher M. Bellitto, Thomas M. Izbicki, and Gerald Christianson, eds., *Introducing Nicholas of Cusa: A Guide to a Renaissance Man* (New York: Paulist Press, 2004), 25–56, and Pauline Moffit Watts, *Nicolaus Cusanus: A Fifteenth-Century Vision of Man*, Studies in the History of Christian Thought XXX (Leiden: E.J. Brill, 1982), 1–14.

[26] This phrase is drawn from Emmanuel Levinas, *Humanism of the Other*, trans. Richard A. Cohen (Urbana: University of Illinois Press, 2003). Trottmann suggests a line of connection between Cusanus and the ethics of Levinas: Christian Trottmann, "La docte ignorance dans le *De Icona*: L'human-isme de l'au dela du concept," in *Nicolas de Cues, Les méthodes d'une pensée. Actes du Colloque de Louvain-la-Neuve*, eds. Jean-Michel Counet and Stéphane Mercier (Louvain-la-Neuve: Collège Érasme, 2005), 105–116, esp. 114–115. We will return to the comparison of Levinas and Nicholas below, but note from the outset that Levinas nowhere discusses Nicholas of Cusa. During Cusanus's time of study in Italy, many works were rediscovered, including works

of the human being was centered in the image of the human face; a reinterpretation of the patristic and scholastic tradition of the *imago Dei*, according to which mankind was created in the image of God.[27] Considering Nicholas as a figure on the threshold of modernity, and debating his role in the birth of the modern world, Hans Blumenberg tended to avoid the spiritual and mystical component of Cusa's writing, despite the textured connection of those themes to his humanism and his scientific speculations.[28] For their part Gadamer and Cassirer recognized the threads binding Cusa's mysti-

---

by Ptolemy, Plutarch, Aristotle and pseudo-Dionysius.

[27] For a discussion of the *imago Dei* tradition, see Michael Edward Moore, "Meditations on the Face in the Middle Ages (With Levinas and Picard)," *Literature and Theology* 24 (2010): 19–37.

[28] Other critics, such as Martin Buber, were strongly attracted to the mystical element in Cusanus. Buber wrote his 1904 dissertation on Cusanus and Jacob Boehme: *Zur Geschichte des Individuationsproblems. Nicolaus von Cues und Jakob Böhme* (PhD diss., University of Vienna, 1904). Translation: "On the History of the Problem of Individuation: Nicholas of Cusa and Jakob Böhme," trans. Sarah Scott, *Graduate Faculty Philosophy Journal* 33 (2012): 371–401. As Sarah Scott explains, "Buber's dissertation discusses Nicholas of Cusa as a figure caught between two epochs and as the first of the modern thinkers of individuality. But in the end Buber sets him aside and moves on to Boehme, because while Nicholas of Cusa gives us the individual, Boehme gives us interdependence" (communication with the author).

cal humanism to his science.[29] Nicholas was not only a scientific thinker, but aspired to the heights of spirituality and hoped to reach the divine: "You raise me up, so that I might be above myself and see beforehand the place of glory to which you invite me."[30] The goal of philosophy was wisdom rather than scientific knowledge.[31] The quest for traces of the incomprehensible divine in nature and in the self was the basic theme of *The Hunt for Wisdom* (written in 1463), and his last work, *The Summit of Contemplation* (1464).[32]

In the distinctive pattern of Cusanus's thought, every center was brought into connection with its periphery, every end with its origins, the Creator with the created. Things of the world were not arranged in a hierarchical cosmos, but were understood as direct witnesses to the absolute.[33] His philosophy freely combined elements of scholastic tradition with the latest trends in humanistic research. His work *De Concordantia Catholica* cast doubt on the authenticity of the *Donation of Constantine*,

---

[29] Ernst Cassirer, *Individual and Cosmos in Renaissance Philosophy*, trans. Mario Domandi (Oxford: Basil Blackwell, 1963), 53.

[30] "Rapis me, ut sim supra me ipsum et praevideam locum gloriae, ad quem me invitas": Nicholas of Cusa, *De Visione*, ed. Riemann, XXV:119, 89.

[31] Vansteenberghe, La *Cardinal Nicolas du Cues*, 424.

[32] *Nicolai de Cusa: Opera Omnia*, vol. 12: *De venatione sapientiae; De apice theoriae*, eds. R. Klibansky and H(ans). G. Senger (Hamburg: In Aedibus Felicis Meiner, 1981). See also Paul Magnard, "La chasse de la sagesse: Une topique de l'oeuvre du Cusain," in *Nicolas de Cues, Les méthodes d'une pensée*, 79–87.

[33] Certeau, "The Gaze: Nicholas of Cusa," 6.

thereby undermining a centuries-old buttress of Roman authority in European politics, and strengthening the independent claims of rising kingdom-states.[34] In response to the Great Schism and the crisis of papal unity, Cusanus argued that Rome should be governed by the common consent of all the faithful as represented by an Ecumenical Council: while insisting that all the faithful should live in unity with the pope: the periphery should be able to guide the center when it has gone astray, but the center must be able to control the periphery. Cusa's legal studies prepared him to engage in discussions of canon law, but this problem of ecclesiastical politics was viewed in a cosmic framework.[35] On one page he sounds like a firebrand, and on the next like a traditionalist.

In his scientific speculations, likewise, the earth was displaced from the center of the cosmos.[36] Cusa came to believe that every point

---

[34] Watanabe shows that Cusa's wide humanistic reading helped him to identify this work as apocryphal: Watanabe, *Political Ideas,* 145–156; Watts connects Cusanus to a "Gothic conciliarist culture of the North": Watts, *Nicolaus Cusanus*, 1. See also Nicholas of Cusa, *The Catholic Concordance*, trans. Paul E. Sigmund (Cambridge, Eng.: Cambridge University Press, 1991), 216–222. On Cusa's politics, see Maurice de Wulf, *History of Mediaeval Philosophy*, trans. Ernest C. Messenger, 2 vols. (London: Longmans, Green and Co., 1925-1926), 2:227–228.

[35] Nicholas of Cusa, *Catholic Concordance*, 76–80. Cusanus's doctrine of *concordantia* attempted to reconcile the doctrine of papal centrality with the supreme authority of an ecumenical council: see Watanabe, *Political Ideas*, 87–95.

[36] This problem has been the subject of decades of

in the universe should be seen as a possible center of the universe, and all points as qualitatively similar.[37] He tried to resolve every conflict of center and edge, unity and multiplicity, with his principle of the *coincidence of opposites*.[38] And Nicholas, although an influential Cardinal at the center of the Church, later took up a difficult post as the Bishop of Brixen, in a narrow alpine valley of the Tyrol, where he had to contend with an aggressive opponent in Sigismund, the Duke of Tyrol, and engage in the reform of small local churches and monasteries. Although he found spiritual allies for his reforms in the monasteries of Melk and Tegernsee, his physical safety was often in jeopardy.[39] Cusanus was an intense thinker and

---

consideration from the perspective of the history of ideas. According to Baron, this epochal insight developed from Cusa's mystical theology rather than from scientific research: Hans Baron, "Toward a More Positive Evaluation of the Fifteenth-Century Renaissance," *Journal of the History of Ideas* 4 (1943): 21–49, esp. 32–34. See the summary in Tamara Albertini, "Mathematics and Astronomy," in Bellitto et al., eds., *Introducing Nicholas of Cusa*, 373–406, esp. 397.

[37] Tom Müller, *"Ut reiecto paschali errore veritati insistamus": Nikolaus von Kues und seine Konzilsschrift* De reparatione kalendarii (Münster: Aschendorff Verlag, 2010), 42.

[38] This is one key area of interest for Blumenberg, *Legitimacy of the Modern Age*, 490–491.

[39] See Morimichi Watanabe, "Nicolaus Cusanus, Monastic Reform in the Tyrol and the *De Visione Dei*," in *Concordia discors. Studi su Niccolò Cusano e l'umanesimo europeo offerti a Giovanni Santinello*, ed. Gregorio Piaia (Padua: Editrice Antenore, 1993), 181–197, and Duclow's summary in Bellitto et al.,

active churchman, who understood the main
currents of thought in his age, and often reflected them in his own writing, attempting to
resolve the apparent contradictions of his age,
with all its political and religious divisions.

eds., *Introducing Nicholas of Cusa*, 38–42. Cusanus
was forced to hire mercenary troops for his defense:
Denys Hay, *Europe in the Fourteenth and Fifteenth
Centuries*, 2d edn. (London: Longman, 1989), 342.

IV. The End of a World Order

During the lifetime of Cusanus, the ideal of European political unity had collapsed in the course of the Hundred Years War, giving way to the rising power of national kingdoms, while at the same time, the Great Schism divided the Church into regional parties favoring rival popes. In the view of early twentieth century historians, "medieval civilization began to crumble, and the formation of the nations announced the dawn of a new world of ideas."[40] The historical com-

---

[40] De Wulf, *History of Mediaeval Philosophy*, 1:29, and Konrad Burdach, *Reformation, Renaissance, Humanismus. Zwei Abhandlungen über die Grundlage moderner Bildung und Sprachkunst* (Berlin: Gebrüder Paetel, 1918), 145. In the view of Hans Baron, the ideal of a divinely sanctioned *sacrum imperium* placed "above historical flux" gave way to "a decentralized history with empires and smaller states all on one level of natural growth and decay": Baron, "Toward a More Positive Evaluation," 36. See also Joachim Leuschner, *Germany in the Late Middle Ages*, trans. Sabine MacCormack (Amsterdam: North-

plex called for reorientation in the realm of principles and interests. The humanist discovery of ancient authors and texts made such a reorientation possible and even attractive. The discovery of ancient monuments and literature was a communal enterprise that spread rapidly, as the allure of knowledge about the distant past caught fire among scholars.[41] The old dream of a sacralized European political order was no longer sustainable, while other political ideals came to the fore, such as the learned mercantile republicanism of Italy. Meanwhile the structures of medieval intellectual life, founded on such traditional educational monuments as the *Sentences* of Peter Lombard, the theologies of Albertus Magnus and Thomas Aquinas, a culture of biblical commentary, and the prestige of Aristotelian metaphysics, were challenged by alternative theologies, the new prominence of ancient writers such as Cicero, and the attractive elegance of humanistic study.[42]

Holland Publishing, 1980), 181.

[41] John Hale, *The Civilization of Europe in the Renaissance* (New York: Athenaeum, 1994), 189–192.

[42] On the political and intellectual world in which Nicholas lived, see Flasch, *Nikolaus von Kues*, 197–242, and Louis Bouyer, *Autour d'Erasme* (Paris: Cerf, 1955), 14–16. In the tradition-minded account of De Wulf, the shared world of ideas served as a "patrimonial factor": De Wulf, *History of Mediaeval Philosophy*, 1:10. The older concept of a Thomist Age was criticized by Oberman, *Dawn of the Reformation*, 4–5. On the continuation of medieval components in Renaissance philosophy, see Paul Oskar Kristeller, "Renaissance Philosophy and the Medieval Tradition," in his *Renaissance Thought and its Sources*, ed. Michael Mooney (New York: Columbia University

Nicholas composed his work *De visione Dei* in 1453, the same year in which Constantinople fell to the Ottoman Turks, an event often held to mark the end of the Middle Ages, a key date in the transition from medieval to modern.[43] Nicholas was left broken-hearted by the fall of the ancient city he knew so well, fearing that precious links to antiquity would be broken.[44] He lamented: "the river of all doctrine is cut off. The fountain of the Muses has run dry. At one moment poetry, at another moment philosophy appears to be entombed."[45] The event however could not dampen the spiritual energy and optimism inspired by humanism,

---

Press, 1979), 106–133.

[43] Roger Aubens and Robert Ricard, *L'Église et la Renaissance (1449-1517)* (Paris: Bloud & Gay, 1951), [=Augustin Fliche and Victor Martin, eds. *Histoire de l'Église depuis les origines jusqu'a nos jours*, Vol. 15], 31. Certeau emphasizes 1453 as a boundary-year: Certeau, "The Gaze: Nicholas of Cusa," 3. See also De Wulf, *History of Mediaeval Philosophy*, 2:261; more profoundly reflecting on the epochal character of this event is Burdach, *Reformation, Renaissance, Humanismus*, 136.

[44] Constantinople the 'ancient city' was seen by many humanists as a living link with the ancient world. Indeed, following the conquest of the city, the Turks destroyed or sold large numbers of ancient manuscripts: see Marios Philippides and Walter K. Hanak, *The Siege and Fall of Constantinople in 1453: Historiography, Topography, and Military Studies* (Farnham: Ashgate, 2011), 195.

[45] "Praecisus est fluvius omnium doctrinarum. Musarum dessicatus est fons. Nunc Poesis, nunc Philosophia sepulta videtur": Epistle of Cusanus, quoted in Bouyer, *Autour d'Erasme*, 27.

which became ever more entrenched, making its way to Rome and the papacy in the person of Nicholas V. Pope Nicholas was another key figure in the transition from medieval to modern concerns: on the one hand, he was the last pope to anoint an emperor in Rome, and on the other hand the first to take an interest in Portuguese voyages of exploration. Nicholas V was a 'Renaissance pope,' the first of many, a great book-collector, and the true first great founder of the Vatican Library.[46] Recognizing a kindred spirit, Pope Nicholas ordained his namesake Nicholas of Cusa as a cardinal.

For his part, Nicholas of Cusa was devoted to the Roman church as the core of doctrinal order and meaning—and to Rome as an ancient seat of culture, during a time when, according to Michel de Certeau "a world [was] coming apart" and familiar sources of unity were dis-

---

[46] Burckhardt saw Nicholas V's lifelong passion for books and book collecting as part of the mainstream of Renaissance humanism: Burckhardt, *Civilization of the Renaissance*, 122. See also Bouyer, *Autour d'Erasme*, 23. On the fall of Byzantium, see Aubens and Ricard, *L'Église et la Renaissance*, 36–37. An early student of Cusanus, Dzieduszycki, believed that the fall of Constantinople undermined the religious optimism associated with humanism: Adalbert Graf Dzieduszycki, "Die Philosophie des Kardinals Nicolaus von Kusa," *Die Kultur* 5 (1904): 29 [24–61]. For a description of Nicholas's library and the variety of influences it assembled, see Voigt, *Wiederbelebung des classischen Alterthums*, 2 vols., 2d edn. (Berlin: Verlag G. Reimer, 1880-1881), 2:206–210. On Nicholas and exploration, see Daniel Waley and Peter Denley, *Later Medieval Europe, 1250-1520*, 3d edn. (Harlow: Longman, 2001), 286.

solving in a "Babelian discord."[47] Nicholas of
Cusa swam against the tides of division and
fearfulness of his age. Even during the collapse
of the medieval world order, and in spite of the
widely known cruelty with which the Turks
sacked Constantinople and killed the inhabit-
ants, Nicholas patiently studied the Qur'an and
explored the continued possibility of interfaith
dialogue.[48] In a period of warlike feelings and
increasing division, he developed a tolerant
humanism that involved an appreciation of the
human body and especially the human face, as
an image of God.[49]

His background connected him to the cultural landscapes of the Rhine and the steep vineyards of the Mosel.[50] Thinking of himself as a
German, he had a strong interest in German
history (becoming involved in the discovery of

---

[47] Certeau, "The Gaze: Nicholas of Cusa," 5.

[48] James E. Biechler, "Interreligious Dialogue," in
Bellitto at al., eds., *Introducing Nicholas of Cusa*, 270–
296. Even on this score there is a medieval backdrop
for Cusanus, of Christian–Moslem scholarly and cultural interaction: see Gebhart, *Origines de la Renaissance*, 185–193.

[49] Nicholas frequently addressed the concept of man
as the image of God [*imago Dei*]: see the texts assembled by Eduard Zellinger, *Cusanus-Konkordanz.
Unter Zugrundelegung der philosophischen und der
bedeutendsten theologischen Werke* (Munich: Max
Heuber Verlag, 1960), 122–123, 128–132.

[50] Certeau highlights the *Germanic* backdrop of
Nicholas's life and writings: Certeau, "The Gaze:
Nicholas of Cusa," 2–6. On the influence of Rhine-
land and lowland mysticism in Cusanus, see Vansteenberghe, *Cardinal Nicolas du Cues*, 426.

the sole manuscript of Tacitus' *Germania*).[51]
The growing humanistic interest in such national histories corresponded to the unraveling
of imperial power, increasing regional divisions
in the Church, and the decline of other interna-
tional sources of political coherence and eco-
nomic order, such as the once-proud Hanseatic
League.[52]

With his quasi-republican views on ecclesiastical politics and his eager hunt for manuscripts to add to his large private library, the
views of Cusanus were very much in keeping
with the Italian humanists whom he knew and
with whom he corresponded. His ideas were
powerfully affected by this community of scholars and their works.[53] He shared their infatua-

---

[51] This type of research illustrates the position of
Cusanus as an exemplary humanist of the period:
see Frank L. Borchardt, *German Antiquity in Renaissance Myth* (Baltimore: Johns Hopkins University
Press, 1971), 40–41. Cusa's discovery of Tacitus was
noted in Paul Lehmann, "The Benedictine Order and
the Transmission of the Literature of Ancient Rome
in the Middle Ages," in his *Erforschung des Mittelalters. Ausgewählte Abhandlungen und Aufsätze*, 5
vols. (Stuttgart: Anton Hiersemann, 1959-1962),
3:173–183, esp. 182. Lehmann contextualized Cusanus in the world of German humanism: "Grundzüge
des Humanismus deutscher Lande zumal im Spiegel
deutscher Bibliotheken des 15. 16. Jahrhunderts,"
5:481–496. Nicholas studied a number of classical
authors, such as Cicero, Pliny, Plautus: Vansteenberghe, *Cardinal Nicolas du Cues*, 19–20.
[52] Waley and Denley, *Later Medieval Europe*, 102.
[53] For an overview of this question, see Pauline M.
Watts, "Renaissance Humanism," in Bellitto et al.,
eds., *Introducing Nicholas of Cusa*, 169–204. On the

tion with classical antiquity and patristic literature, and the intensive critical atmosphere of
humanistic scholarship.[54] His passion for old
books, however, led him to adopt some uncon-
ventional ideas, as Nicholas explained: "Not
without considerable diligence, I assembled many
original works, for a long time fallen out of use,
in the libraries of old monasteries."[55] According
to his own account, these old books led him to
develop the novel doctrines of his *Catholic Concordance* in favor of summoning a great Council to resolve the discord in the church. Following this hint, one might offer an initial thesis,
that ancient books held the key to cultural and
historical transfiguration, and paradoxically, the
appearance of modernity.

Nicholas was accepted as part of the Italian
scene. Indeed, Marsilio Ficino (1433-1499), head
of the Platonic Academy in Florence, considered him an avatar of a hallowed line of sages
going back to Plato and pseudo-Dionysius.[56]
Modern historians saw things otherwise. De-

---

contents of Nicholas's library, see Watts, *Nicolaus
Cusanus,* 13–24. See also Vansteenberghe, *Cardinal
Nicolas du Cues*, 18–21, and the brilliant work of
Giuseppe Saitta, *Nicolò Cusano e l'umanisimo italiano*
(Bologna: Tamari Editori, 1957), 19–20.

[54] "L'atmosfera critica," in which the study of antiquity led away from received texts and accepted ideas:
Saitta, *Nicolò Cusano*, 14.

[55] "Originalia enim multa, longe ab usu perdita, per
veterum coenobiorum armaria non sine magna dili-
genti collegi": text cited in Saitta, *Nicolò Cusano*, 15;
see also Bellitto et al., eds., *Introducing Nicholas of
Cusa*, 174.

[56] Stefan Swiezawski, *Histoire de la philosophie européenne au XVe siècle* (Paris: Beauchesne, 1990), 14.

spite the fact that Cusanus had been lionized in Florence, he had no place in the foundational historical study of the Renaissance by Jacob Burckhardt, for whom the Renaissance was an exclusively Italian affair, with classically-inspired art in the cities of Florence, Venice and Rome as its highest expression. The history of art, humanistic scholarship and culture prevailed over other historical factors in the developing interest in the Renaissance and the origins of modern times.

V. The Faces of Nicholas of Cusa

Like other philosophers of the Quattrocento, Cusanus drew inspiration from the radiant structures of neoplatonism.[57] Other of his ideas were more unique, and disquieting for his contemporaries, such as his belief in the "coincidence of opposites" (*coincidentia oppositorum*), a principle that appeared to violate one of the basic pillars of philosophy, the law of identity.[58] As we have seen, he relied on this principle to balance papal and conciliar authority: the coincidence of ruler and ruled. A striking illustration of this concept appears in Cusa's work from the epochal year 1453, *On the Vision of God/De visione Dei*.[59] This treatise, which later

---

[57] Gadamer recognized a core of Christian platonism in Cusa's writings: Gadamer, *Truth and Method*, 438.

[58] "La *coincidentia oppositorum*, pièce la plus inquiétante du systeme": Bouyer, *Autour d'Erasme*, 62.

[59] Nicholas of Cusa, *De Visione*, ed. Riemann; translation in *Complete Philosophical and Theological Treatises of Nicholas of Cusa*, trans. Jasper Hopkins, 2

figured in the twentieth-century philosophical debates regarding Cusanus, set out to reveal the human face as an image of God. At the same time, this was a work of mystical theology, *mystica theologia*, much in keeping with the *Letter on Mystical Theology* he wrote for the monks of Tegernsee in the same year.[60]

Composed as a letter to the monks of Tegernsee, *De visione Dei* began with a prayer that the ideas to be expounded might be made comprehensible to the monks, as he intended to lead them "into most sacred darkness."[61] The treatise is a demonstration, or spiritual exercise, based on an "omnivoyant" painting—i.e., a portrait whose eyes seem to follow the viewer around the room, and to look at every viewer from any angle: "through subtle pictorial artistry, [the face in the painting] is such that it seems to behold everything around it. There are in existence many of these excellently depicted faces": Cusanus mentions a painting of an archer in Nuremberg, a self-portrait of Rogier Van der Weyden in Brussels, and a painting of an angel in Brixen."[62] Unfortunately all

---

vols. (Minneapolis: J. Banning Press, 2001), 679–743 [cited hereafter as *Vision of God*, trans. Hopkins].

[60] Edmond Vansteenberghe, trans., *La Vision de Dieu par le Cardinal Nicolas de Cuse (1401-1464)* (Louvain: Éditions de Museum Lessianum, 1925), xv. Rudolf Stadelmann, *Vom Geist des ausgehenden Mittelalters* (1929; repr. Stuttgart: Friedrich Frommann Verlag [Günther Holzboog], 1966), 103.

[61] "In sacratissimam obscuritatem manuducere": Nicholas of Cusa, *De visione Dei*, ed. Riemann, Praef. 1, 4; *Vision of God*, trans. Hopkins, 680.

[62] Nicholas of Cusa, *De visione Dei*, ed. Riemann,

of the paintings he mentions are now lost.[63]

Nicholas announced that along with the treatise he was sending the monks just such a painting, entitled "An Icon of God." Presumably we should imagine a familiar type of late medieval painting, in which Christ appears to gaze directly outward at the viewer, in mildness or sorrow.[64] An alternative title for the book is *De*

---

[63] Praef. 2, 5; *Vision of God*, trans. Hopkins, 680.

[63] Panofsky suggested that the self-portrait of Van der Weyden was copied into a tapestry (the Tapisserie d'Herkenbald) in Brussels: Erwin Panofsky, "*Facies illa Rogeri maximi pictoris*," in *Late Classical and Mediaeval Studies in Honor of Albert Mathias Friend*, ed. Kurt Weitzmann (Princeton: Princeton University Press, 1955), 392–400. See the discussion in Certeau, "The Gaze: Nicholas of Cusa," 11n10, 11n11, and Cassirer, *Individual and Cosmos*, 31. Panofsky's suggestion was not supported by later study: see Micheline Sonkes, *Dessins du XVe siècle. Groupe van der Weyden, Essai de catalogue des originaux du maître, des copies et des dessins anonymes inspireés par son style* (Brussels: Centre National de Recherches, 1969), 22, 238.

[64] Portraits of Christ were a common theme in northern painting of the late Middle Ages, fulfilling a desire to "look [the] Saviour in the eye for a moment": Meyer Schapiro, *Words and Pictures: On the Literal and the Symbolic in the Illustration of a Text* (The Hague: Mouton, 1973), 39. Bond suggests that the icon might have been a painting of Veronica with her veil: H. Lawrence Bond, "The 'Icon' and the 'Iconic Text'," in *Nicholas of Cusa and his Age: Intellect and Spirituality: Essays Dedicated to the Memory of F. Edward Cranz, Thomas P. McTighe and Charles Trinkaus*, ed. Thomas M. Izbicki, Studies in the History of Christian Thought 105 (Leiden: Brill, 2002), 181–182 [177–197]. See also Henk van Os et al., *The*

icona Dei: that is, a book about an icon of Christ's face. Nevertheless, the treatise functions just as well without the presence of such an icon. The purpose was to lead the reader through a spiritual exercise. Thus the work deliberately blurs the line between original vision and *ekphrasis*, and lays out the stages of a guided meditation or mental game.[65] He instructed the monks to hang the painting on the north wall of the chapel and observe it together.

"Regardless of the place from which each of you looks at it, each will have the impression that he alone is being looked at by it." As you move about the chapel, he explained, the gaze of the icon will follow you.[66] The face itself is

---

Art of Devotion in the Late Middle Ages in Europe, 1300-1500 (Princeton: Princeton University Press, 1994), 40–45, and (with reproductions) David Conway, "A Head of Christ by John Van Eyck," *The Burlington Magazine* 39 (1921): 253–255, 257, 260. It is unclear to me why Panofsky suggested that, "in a Northern painting of 1449 a face looking out of the picture was too startling a novelty to be overlooked by even a philosopher": Panofsky, *"Facies illa Rogeri maximi pictoris,"* 396.

[65] There was an ancient tradition of ekphrasis of an imagined image, as in Homer's description of the shield of Achilles, *Iliad*, Book 18. Such a nonexistent picture of God might also fall into the category of *acheiropoietos*, an icon not made by human hands. Compare with Bond, "The 'Icon' and the 'Iconic Text'," 182.

[66] Nicholas of Cusa, *De visione Dei*, ed. Riemann, Praef. 3, 5; *Vision of God*, trans. Hopkins, 680–681. Schapiro, *Words and Pictures*, points to significant antecedents for the comparison of God to an omni-

immobile: an *immobilis facies*, but it will seem to follow each person with an equal, private, and intimate gaze. This picture, or the spiritual exercise based on the picture, Nicholas hoped, would lead the monks to the gates of mystic theology.[67]

The spiritual exercise could now begin. The monks should consider that like all human beings, we are limited and confined to a certain place and region, and that there is a limit to what we can see. But the God who looks at us has a perfection of sight that is unconfined and takes in everything at once. The Absolute Sight of God is the uncanny reality that is only imperfectly represented in the painted gaze of the icon. The Absolute Gaze is actually livingly able to follow each person. Haas comments: "God is, so to speak, a reader," who takes in every individual thing with a *single* glance (*unico intuitu*).[68] Up to this point, this seems to be a typical medieval complexity. But Nicholas goes on to suggest that God's ability to see is involved in our own capacity for vision: "Absolute sight is present in all seeing."[69] Vision is the openness of things to being seen, an openness in the heart of being in which we participate. Our own looking is a portion of God's looking. The effort to imagine and 'picture' God thus becomes an attempt to imagine and 'picture' the self and its relation to God.[70]

---

voyant image (60n79).

[67] Certeau, "The Gaze: Nicholas of Cusa," 12.

[68] Haas, *Deum mistice videre*, 36.

[69] Nicholas of Cusa, *De visione Dei*, ed, Riemann, cap. II, 12; *Vision of God*, trans. Hopkins, 683.

[70] Bond, "The 'Icon' and the 'Iconic Text'," 184.

God's unconfined vision is like that represented by the painted illusion of panoptic vision in the icon.[71] The monks should understand that God's gaze is everywhere and that the eyes and love of God can be felt sweeping over and through one. At this point, the spiritual exercise could go one step further, to consider this icon hanging in the chapel as a vision of God's face. This was something to be seen 'intellectually,' and to serve as a kind of mirror. God's face, present to the mind, is the culmination of the concept: it is "the Exemplar of each and every face," and yet goes beyond all faces. God's face is the original of all human faces. And from this Cusanus drew some remarkable implications: "all faces have beauty, but they are not beauty itself (*pulchritudo*). But your face, O Lord, has beauty and this having is being."[72] This lovely expression was a departure from patristic and scholastic tradition, which had interpreted the human likeness to God as confined to the invisible realm of the virtues or the character of the soul, excluding the body. According to Cusanus, all human faces are beautiful, because of their reflection of the divine ex-

---

[71] Vision is basic to Cusa's concept of deity. Nicholas was intrigued by the derivation of the Latin *Deus* from the Greek *theos*, which implies vision. In the fragment *De Theologicis complementis*, Nicholas explained, "Deus enim a theos dicitur, quod est videre, quia omnia videt": *De Theologicis com-plementis cap. 12*, edited (anonymously) in *Concordia discors*, 233 [233–235]. See discussion in Certeau, "The Gaze: Nicholas of Cusa," 23.

[72] Nicholas of Cusa, *De visione Dei*, ed. Riemann, cap. VI, 22; *Vision of God*, trans. Hopkins, 689.

emplar. God's face is the *face of faces*: "In all faces the Face of faces is seen in veiled and symbolic manner."[73] Divine unity is the foundation of human multiplicity. Once awakened to this, the monks should be able to observe the Face of faces in themselves and others, experiencing an intense moment of contemplation—a "certain secret and hidden silence."[74]

God turns toward humankind and offers himself. "We embrace our likeness because we are shown ourselves" in an image, and we learn to love ourselves with its help.[75] The one who follows this spiritual exercise will thereby come to understand that all people share a single humanity: "it is present to one man as much as to another." As Nicholas explains: "humanity does not abandon people, whether they are moved or not moved, whether they are sleeping or resting." God himself is this unrestricted humanity, "Absolute Humanity."[76] Asking the monks finally to contemplate their own faces, Cusanus invites them to say: "Lord god, Enlightener of hearts, my face is a true face." The truth resides not only in the exemplar but in the very human *image*, which Nicholas calls a

---

[73] "In omnibus faciebus videtur facies facierum velate et in aenigmate": Nicholas of Cusa, *De visione Dei*, ed. Riemann, cap. VI, 22; *Vision of God*, trans. Hopkins, 689.

[74] "In quoddam secretum et occultum silentium": Nicholas of Cusa, *De visione Dei*, ed. Riemann, cap. VI, 22; *Vision of God*, Hopkins, 689.

[75] Bond, "The 'Icon' and the 'Iconic Text'," 192–193.

[76] "Homo . . . absolutus": Nicholas of Cusa, *De visione Dei*, ed. Riemann, cap. IX, 32–33; *Vision of God*, trans. Hopkins, 695–696 [translation altered here].

"facial truth"—"my face is true insofar as it is an image."[77] So here was expounded a quite remarkable vision of humanity that would validate the visible appearance and existence of every particular human being, a humanism of the human face.

With this discussion of the human face, Cusanus seems to confirm Jacob Burckhardt's thesis regarding the emergence of self-consciousness and individuality in the Renaissance. However, *De visione Dei* is a deeply religious, christocentric treatise. The humanism of Cusanus was thoroughly grounded in his religion. Chiffoleau would suggest that a mixture of humanism and mysticism reveals the very modernity of fifteenth-century religion.[78]

---

[77] "Facies mea vera est facies": Nicholas of Cusa, *De visione Dei*, ed. Riemann, cap. XV, 53; *Vision of God*, trans. Hopkins, 710–711.

[78] Jacques Chiffoleau, *La religion flamboyante. France, 1320-1520* (Paris: Éditions Points, 2011), 167–169.

VI. Renaissance Studies

The humanism prevailing in the treatise *On the Vision of God* combines mystical elements with an appreciation of human actuality. In this way Cusa's theology expresses an awareness of human individuality that was just coming to the fore in the Renaissance, and which was, to many historians and philosophers, a modern phenomenon, representing a liberation from the communal norms of medieval society. Over the course of the twentieth century, as we shall see, Cusanus scholars and historians often discussed the role of Nicholas of Cusa as a harbinger of modernity. The concept of modernity, and other factors in the debate, such as humanism, were extensively developed in historical scholarship on Renaissance history. Only a few landmarks can be noted here.

The philosophical debate over modernity and the role of Nicholas of Cusa drew on the latest historical research into the Renaissance and the origins of the modern world. These historians tended to sketch the Renaissance and the origins of modernity in broad strokes, embracing such topics as the history of individual consciousness, the rise of natural science, the humanistic study of antiquity, and the discovery of artistic naturalism and perspective.[79] The arts had a prominent position in historical writing on the Renaissance, in a period when Europeans and Americans alike had begun to flock to Italy to admire the art and architecture of the Renaissance cities, as a reaction against a certain emptiness felt to exist in modern urban and industrialized landscapes.[80]

An examination of the debate over the modernity of Nicholas of Cusa invites us to explore this older base of erudition. The intimate connection between historical scholarship and the western philosophical tradition means that historical literature of the late-nineteenth and early twentieth centuries can illuminate contemporary philosophical debates. Conversely, historians were often preoccupied with philosophical questions. Frequently the relevant works are formidable examples of scholarship, evoking fascination with their worn leather bindings and patterned endpapers. The brown pag-

---

[79] The Renaissance was often characterized as the discovery of an ancient ideal, un idéal antique, that awakened desire for personal liberation: Aubens and Ricard, L'Église et la Renaissance, 205.

[80] Berndt Roeck, Florence 1900: The Quest for Arcadia, trans. Stuart Spencer (New Haven: Yale University Press, 2009), with much information about German visitors, especially Aby Warburg. For American visitors, see Van Wyck Brooks, The Dream of Arcadia: American Artists and Writers in Italy, 1760-1915 (New York: Dutton, 1958).

es, with their fragrance of cedar, embody several layers of time and meaning. The volumes convey the historical character of modernity, and the networks of time embedded in this concept. These books can be quite touching, too, because of their devotion to values such as independence of mind, creative freedom, and political liberty, whose origins, it was believed, could be traced back to the Renaissance.[81]

At the same time, debate over the proper direction for contemporary philosophy took the form of a search for modern origins. A consensus had formed that the origins of modernity lay in the Renaissance period. The influential work of Jacob Burckhardt had defined the Renaissance so convincingly that later historians and philosophers took his work as the starting point for all further discussion, as is still frequently the case.

Originally an historian's concept, modernity (and the Renaissance) became for philosophers a problem in the history of philosophy and thus a structural component in the history of European historical consciousness.[82] The philos-

---

[81] Writing in the Third Republic, Gebhart readily identified France with these values (and located their origins partly in medieval France): Gebhart, *Origines de la Renaissance en Italie*, 41.

[82] The history of Renaissance scholarship was often involved in questions of epochal change or periodization: Paul Oskar Kristeller, "Humanism and Scholasticism in the Italian Renaissance," in Kristeller, *Renaissance Thought*, 85–105. This became a general theme of historiography, the most influential being Heussi's wide-ranging "genetic analysis": Karl Heussi, *Altertum, Mittelalter und Neuzeit in der Kirchenges-*

ophers studied historical treatises, and undertook their own somewhat limited and idiosyncratic historical investigations, focusing on the
history of ideas and what can be called the *epos*
of European historical consciousness. In this
way, questions of cosmology, the stature of
metaphysics, and the history of science came to
the fore, and interest was kindled in the writings of Nicholas of Cusa. This would displace
Petrarch (1304-1374), who for most historians
reflected the highpoint of the Renaissance, and
the role of art as the paradigmatic expression of
the Renaissance. Unlike the masterful, solitary
figure of Petrarch, Nicholas of Cusa (1401-
1464) was a very different type of person—a man
of affairs, a cardinal of the Church, a lawyer,
philosopher and theologian with a mystical
and conjectural turn of mind.[83] Like Petrarch,
Cusanus was a humanist, having extensive knowledge
of the past, and an instinctive awareness of antiquity, although mathematics and speculative
philosophy became his chief legacy. These interests explain why, at first, the existence of
Cusanus was barely recorded in scholarship on
the Renaissance.

Georg Voigt's *Die Wiederbelebung des classischen Alterthums*, first published in 1859, was
one of the great early brilliant accounts of the
rediscovery of antiquity and ancient literature

---

*chichte. Ein Beitrag zum Problem der historischen
Periodisierung* (1921; repr. Darmstadt: Wissenschaftliche Buchgesellschaft, 1969).

[83] Watts, *Nicolaus Cusanus*, 1. Dzieduszycki cloyingly
calls Cusanus a "purple-clad philosopher," *purpur
bekleidete Philosoph*: Dzieduszycki, "Philosophie des
Kardinals Nicholaus," 29.

during the Renaissance. According to Voigt, humanism was the very essence of the Renaissance period, although its authors sometimes fell short of their lofty aspirations with dull, imitative writings.[84] Attempting a complete study of Renaissance mentality within the confines of literature and the arts, Voigt developed an attractive and convincing portrait of humanism. As he explained, in the writings and activities of Petrarch a new cultural configuration was crystallized: "no chasm seems to lie between Dante and Petrarch, insofar as the latter could have seen the old master when he was a young man. However, in terms of education (*Bildung*) and form of life they were quite divided."[85] Voigt detailed the accomplishments of Renaissance scholars and artists in his careful studies of humanistic activity in Milan, Siena, Florence and Rome. According to Voigt, the distinctive character of Renaissance humanism was based on its revival of ancient literature and its liberation of the individual. This occurred long before Nicholas of Cusa came on the scene, and consequently Cusa received little attention, despite Voigt's extensive familiarity with humanism north of the Alps.[86]

Following the impressive and widely-read

---

[84] Wallace K. Ferguson, *The Renaissance in Historical Thought: Five Centuries of Interpretation* (Cambridge, Eng.: Riverside Press, 1948), 160.

[85] Georg Voigt, *Die Wiederbelebung des classischen Alterthums*, 2 vols., 2d edn. (Berlin: Verlag G. Reimer, 1880-1881), 1:16. See also Ferguson, *The Renaissance in Historical Thought*, 159–163.

[86] Voigt, *Wiederbelebung des classischen Alterthums*, 2:264–317.

work of Voigt, Renaissance studies frequently grappled with serious questions of periodization and historical meaning.[87] Far more influential and stylistically intense than Voigt was the work of Jacob Burckhardt, who helped to define the practice of cultural history, and whose *Civilization of the Renaissance in Italy* remains a prominent thesis about the nature of the Renaissance and the character of modernity. Perceiving the interwoven texture of numerous historical factors: painting and sculpture, poetry, history-writing and political life, Burckhardt developed the methods of cultural history in order to account for them.[88]

Burckhardt wished to identify the origins of modernity, but not because he admired the modern world, as did many historians. He believed that the Renaissance epoch had set in motion the mechanisms of a terrible future. Reacting against the character of modernity, Burckhardt issued dire warnings, believing that Europe would witness a collapse of its civilization in a series of wars.[89] In response to this

---

[87] A summary of these questions exists in Heussi's valuable handbook. As he demonstrates, the turn from medieval to modern can only be established in the context of debates over extrinsic cultural, intellectual or religious criteria, such as "individualism." There are no objective historical periods: Heussi, *Altertum, Mittelalter und Neuzeit*, 41.

[88] The origin of Jacob Burckhardt's cultural-historical methods is brilliantly discussed in Felix Gilbert, "Jacob Burckhardt's Student Years: The Road to Cultural History," *Journal of the History of Ideas* 47 (1986): 249–274.

[89] He believed that "the established political forms of the greatest civilized peoples are tottering or chang-

sense of crisis, he adopted a personal ethos of austere devotion to research and "teaching as a way of life."[90] Despite its world-historical implications, for Burckhardt the Renaissance was nevertheless a strictly Italian affair.[91]

Writing in 1860, Burckhardt argued that the city of Florence was the birthplace of the modern age: as we see them in the Renaissance, "the Florentines are the pattern and the earliest type of . . . modern Europeans generally."[92] The modernity of Florence and the Italian Renaissance consisted of the following: the most modern institutions and activities were

ing": Jacob Burckhardt, "On Fortune and Misfortune in History," in Jacob Burckhardt, *Reflections on History* (Indianapolis: Liberty Classics, 1979), 340. See the discussion in Hans Blumenberg, *Shipwreck with Spectator: Paradigm of a Metaphor for Existence*, trans. Steven Rendall (Cambridge, Mass.: MIT Press, 1997), 67–73. On Burckhardt's medievalism, see Lewis W. Spitz, "Reflections on Early and Late Humanism: Burckhardt's Morality and Religion," in *Jacob Burckhardt and the Renaissance 100 Years After* (Lawrence: University of Kansas Museum of Art, 1960), 15–27, esp. 23.

[90] Burckhardt's ethos became neo-humanism and *Bildung* in a spirit of "ascetic self-mastery": John R. Hinde, *Jacob Burckhardt and the Crisis of Modernity* (Montreal: McGill-Queen's University Press, 2000), 135.

[91] Lionel Gossman, *Basel in the Age of Burckhardt: An Age of Unseasonable Ideas* (Chicago: University of Chicago Press, 2000). The term Renaissance, with its biblical connotation of moral rebirth, was first used in Italy: Burdach, *Reformation, Renaissance, Humanismus*, 14–19.

[92] Jacob Burckhardt, *The Civilization of the Renaissance in Italy*, 3d edn. (London: Phaidon, 2006), 58.

developed in the Italian city-states, alongside the concomitant idea that politics should and could be shaped by human art.[93]

Whereas medieval man had been conscious of himself "only as a member of a race, people, party, family, or corporation," during the Renaissance "man became a spiritual individual."[94] With humanism, subjectivity came to the fore, along with a dignified conception of a shared humanity.[95] The importance of human history was rediscovered: an awareness of living and dead humankind.[96] Renaissance humanism was a portentous movement that gave birth to the modern world.[97] According to Burckhardt, crowning all these changes was the poet Petrarch, "one of the first truly modern men," because of his recognition of nature as described in

---

[93] Burckhardt, *Civilization of the Renaissance*, 58–59. See Roberta Garner, "Jacob Burckhardt as a Theorist of Modernity: Reading *The Civilization of the Renaissance in Italy*," *Sociological Theory* 8 (1990): 51–52 [48–57].

[94] Burckhardt, *Civilization of the Renaissance*, 87.

[95] Self-awareness and self-consciousness are basic components of Burckhardt's "identification of modernity with individualism" (Garner, "Jacob Burckhardt," 50).

[96] This theme was supported in Becker's view of Renaissance humanism as transforming archaic social bonds, spelling the end of traditional society in Europe: Marvin B. Becker, *Civility and Society in Western Europe, 1300-1600* (Bloomington: Indiana University Press, 1988).

[97] Burckhardt, *Civilization of the Renaissance*, 231. For Baron this was the discovery of a human-centered history and a horizontal view of states: Baron, "Toward a More Positive Evaluation," 37.

the *Ascent of Mt. Ventoux*.[98] The image of Petrarch as the founder of humanism and the first
embodiment of the modern spirit would be
further developed in works like Pierre de Nolhac's *Petrarque et l'humanisme*, which supported
the historical significance of Petrarch as a literary figure with extensive studies of Petrarch's
library and autograph manuscripts.[99] Nolhac's
meticulous reconstruction of Petrarch's scholarly activities and literary accomplishments con-
firmed his stature as "the first modern man,"
who had "escaped almost entirely the influence
of his age and milieu," an eccentric figure, writing in the solitude of Provence, who was nevertheless able to change the character of history.[100]

For the critic Konrad Burdach, an adherent
of the methods of *Geistesgeschichte*, the concept of humanism was too vague and broad as
Voigt and Burckhardt used it: as such the term
might very well indicate the entire range of
phenomena regarding the revival and appreciation of Greco-Roman literature, science, art and
Latinity. If that were the case, it could even be
said that the character of modernity was entire-

---

[98] Burckhardt, *Civilization of the Renaissance*, 192;
although it has been suggested that the inwardness
of Petrarch's religious response at the summit of Mt.
Ventoux does not readily correspond to Burckhardt's
view: Hale, *Civilization of Europe*, 534; this is similar
to the view of Blumenberg.

[99] Pierre de Nolhac, *Petrarque et l'humanisme d'après
un essai de restitution de sa bibliothèque* (Paris: É.
Bouillon, 1892).

[100] Pierre de Nolhac, *Petrarque et l'humanisme*, 2 vols.,
2d edn. (Paris: Honoré Champion, 1907), 1:2.

ly and essentially humanistic. According to Burdach the aristocratic ideals of the Renaissance were largely responsible for shaping the character of European political and social culture. It was still possible to assert this in 1918, when the classical German educational tradition of *Bildung* still retained its prestige.[101]

Burdach raised a major criticism of Burckhardt and Voigt: that revivals of Roman antiquity had occurred repeatedly before the so-called Renaissance, all through the Middle Ages, when knowledge of classical Latin authors was splendidly revived in Irish, Carolingian, Anglo-Saxon, Ottonian, French, Cassino-Roman, Norse, and Staufen *renaissances*.[102] Such a multiplicity of renascences implied that knowledge of ancient literature returned again and again, in a long-enduring wave pattern whereby periods of forgetfulness were followed by intense periods of literary activity and cultural retrieval. This was to suggest that modernity was shaped long before the so-called Renaissance, that modernity was in fact *medieval*.

---

[101] Burdach, *Reformation, Renaissance, Humanismus*, 104–105.

[102] "Es gab in diesem Sinn während der mittelalterlichen Jahrhunderte eine irische, eine karolingishce, eine altenglische, eine ottonische, eine französische, eine cassinesisch-römische, eine normannische, eine staufische Renaissance des römischen Altertums". Burdach, *Reformation, Renaissance, Humanismus*, 139.

VII. Medieval Civilization and Modernity

Writing in Burckhardt's Basel in the early 1920s, Ernst Walser rejected the neat division of Medieval, Renaissance and Modern periods "von denen eine jede ihren charakteristischen Ideenkomplex aufzuweisen hat."[103] Rather than looking for renaissances in the Middle Ages, Walser discovered medieval continuities extending into the Renaissance. Walser's studies in the history of humanistic scholarship convinced him that the Middle Ages had already witnessed several episodic revivals of the study of ancient literature. Certainly the Renaissance battle-cry *Ad fontes* ("back to the sources") indi-

---

[103] From Walser's *Studien zur Weltanschauung der Renaissance* (Basel: Benno Schwabe, 1920), reprinted in a collection of Walser's works, with an introductory essay by Werner Kaegi: Ernst Walser, *Gesammelte Studien zur Geistesgeschichte der Renaissance* (Basel: Verlag von Benno Schwabe & Co., 1932), 98.

cated the humanist abandonment of scholasticism and an ardent turn to antiquity, paving the way for modern secularization. But Walser suggested that for all his apparent originality, the significant scholarly labors of Petrarch were only a further development of work going on long before the Renaissance—Petrarch's humanism was in essence no different than the humanisms of the Carolingian and Ottonian Renaissances. No boundary between medieval and Renaissance could be drawn: "Mit tausend Fäden spinnt das Alte zum Neuen sich weiter."[104] The story was of modern continuity with the medieval period. The Renaissance opened no radically new mental orientation, undertook no modernization of religion, in fact: "all the humanists, poets and thinkers from the fourteenth to the sixteenth century remained 'loyal medieval orthodox' sons of the Church."[105] Another unstated implication of this view is that it transferred the origins of modernity from the sun-drenched city-states of Italy to a colder gothic, German north.

Walser was familiar with Johan Huizinga's cultural history of 1919, *The Autumn of the Middle Ages*, with its bleak vision of the fifteenth century as an age of 'dark sadness,' scarred by outbursts of hatred, assassination and contra-

---

[104] Walser, *Gesammelte Studien*, 118. Perhaps there is an echo here of Konrad Burdach, who saw that humanism and the Renaissance emerged "out of the necessity of the age": "Durch starke Fäden hängen sie mit dem Mittelalter zusammen," and to the modern period as well: Burdach, *Reformation, Renaissance, Humanismus*, 143.

[105] Walser, *Gesammelte Studien*, 125.

dictions, the last flaming embers of a civilization, when "so intense and colorful was life that
it could stand the mingling of the smell of
blood and roses."[106] Like Burdach and Walser,
Huizinga was similarly critical of Burckhardt's
image of the Renaissance as a period of rebirth
and commencement, seeing it instead as a time
of historical closure, the end of an age of social
stability and religious certainty.[107] For Huizinga,
Nicholas of Cusa was only a world-abandoning
mystic like Eckhart and Ruusbroec, in tune
with the *devotio moderna*, which was a reaction
against all systems of theology in favor of "pre-
intellectual spiritual life."[108] Writing in 1929,
the northerner Johan Nordström likewise con-
firmed the idea that the Renaissance was really
a continuation of medieval trends, an uninter-
rupted arc extending from the Italian classicism

---

[106] Johann Huizinga, *The Autumn of the Middle Ages*,
trans. Rodney J. Payton and Ulrich Mammitzsch
(Chicago: University of Chicago Press, 1996), 24. See
also the discussion of Huizinga in Walser, *Gesammelte Studien*, 310.

[107] Ferguson, *The Renaissance in Historical Thought*,
373–376.

[108] Huizinga, *Autumn of the Middle Ages*, 265–266. A
similar point is made in Heer's passionate and un-
timely *Europäische Geistesgeschichte* of 1953: "Each
of Cusa's ideas can be translated into a political an-
swer to some burning question affecting the empire,
the Church, Europe, or the individual conscience"
(Friedrich Heer, *The Intellectual History of Europe*,
trans. Jonathan Steinberg [Cleveland: World Publishing Co., 1966], 195). This brilliant work responds to
much earlier discussions: it was delayed by Heer's
wartime imprisonment and the fact that his papers
were destroyed by the Nazis.

of the *trecento* to the *quattrocento*, and especially in France, artistic and literary achievements
from the twelfth century onward.[109] This showed that modernity could be rooted in northern
and gothic developments.

The emphasis on the Italian Renaissance by
historians such as Voigt and Burckhardt had left
northern Europe largely to one side, with nei-
ther conceptual space for a northern Renaissance, nor for any consideration of Nicholas of
Cusa. Johannes Janssen sought to bring northern history of the fifteenth century to the fore
in his massive history of late medieval German
cultural and religious history.[110] Janssen por-
trayed Nicholas of Cusa as someone who bridged
the spirit of the Middle Ages and the new cultural framework of this ultramontane Renaissance. As a humanist, Cusanus helped to intro-
duce the knowledge of ancient literature to
Germany, thereby paving the way for the German Renaissance and its humanists, such as
Beatus Rhenanus, Rudolf Agricola, and Trithe-
mius, all of whom had been overlooked in studies
centering the Renaissance in Italy. As Janssens
noted, Cusanus was an enthusiastic early pro-
ponent of the printing press, and thus should
be seen as an important, characteristic humanist. In his attempts to reform the Church, and

---

[109] This work was translated in 1933: Johan Nordström, *Moyen Âge et Renaissance. Essai historique*,
trans. T. Hammar (Paris: Librairie Stock, 1933), 181.

[110] Johannes Janssen, *Geschichte des deutschen Volkes
seit dem Ausgang des Mittelalters*, 8 vols. (Freiburg im
Breisgau: Herder, 1879-1894). Abridged translation
into French: Jean Janssen, *L'Allemagne à la fin du
Moyen Âge* (Paris: E. Plon, Nourrit et Cie., 1887).

in his transformation of the mental world, meanwhile, Cusanus helped pave the way for the Reformation, like other great figures of late medieval theology such as Gabriel Biel and Geiler de Kaiserberg.[111] Thus here was a new blending of themes in which a northern Renaissance was connected to the appearance of the Protestant Reformation in northern lands.

Up until this time, Janssen was unusual in tracing a northern Renaissance so as to include the humanist scholars of Alsace and Germany. Historians of the German-speaking world preferred to focus on the Reformation, rather than the Renaissance, as the great cultural upheaval bringing the Middle Ages and its religion to an end. Hans von Schubert made this explicit in a vinegary essay, "Reformation und Humanismus," published in 1924: "Deutschland hatte keine Renaissance, die den Namen gedient."[112] Schubert maintained that Burckhardt's concept of a Renaissance could never be applied to German history, given the fact that northerners remained devotedly bound to the medieval Christian past right up until the explosive moment of the Lutheran revolution. German history moves directly from Middle Ages to Reformation without passing through a Renaissance like that of Italy. The historical space of modernity and its Renaissance origins remained vague and ill-defined. Many scholars saw a tur-

---

[111] Janssen, *L'Allemagne à la fin du Moyen Âge*, 1–5, 101.

[112] Carl Neumann, quoting Von Schubert, in "Ranke und Burckhardt und die Geltung des Begriffes 'Renaissance' insbesondere für Deutschland," *Historische Zeitschrift* 150 (1934): 490 [485–496].

bulent sense of *ending* and *cultural transfor-*
mation in the fifteenth century, either the collapse of rotten wood, or the emergence of
something enduring and new.

Burckhardt's view of the Renaissance remained influential, providing the background
for the eclectic scholarship and darker historical vision of Aby Warburg (1866-1929) who
likewise asserted the uniqueness of an Italian
Renaissance and its connection to antiquity.
This understanding of the Renaissance drew
explicitly on Jacob Burckhardt, who was the
"secular patron saint" of the Warburg Library.[113]
For Warburg the Renaissance was a unique
period in which stark polarities stood in conflict. The restoration of antiquity was never a
calm appreciation of the past, but an agony of
contending influences. Modernity emerged as a
series of forces welling up out of antiquity.[114]
These forces awakened a struggle for enlightenment against older, fearful demonic strata
stemming from the ancient past. This was no
orderly arrival of modernism, progress or tech-

---

[113] Hans Liebeschütz, "Aby Warburg (1866-1929) as
Interpreter of Civilisation," in *Leo Baeck Institute
Yearbook* XVI (1971): 234 [225–236].

[114] Silvia Ferretti, *Cassirer, Panofsky, and Warburg:
Symbol, Art and History* (New Haven: Yale University
Press, 1989), 70–76. According to Liebeschütz, nei-
ther did Warburg conceive of the medieval period as
a coherent civilization, but a "borderland without
rights of its own." Warburg focused on post-medieval
cultural trends, and the emergence of the "forces of
Antiquity" in fifteenth-century Florence: Liebeschütz,
"Aby Warburg," 229. Liebeschütz for his part was an
interpeter of the culture and ideas of the Middle
Ages.

nology, but already a modernity of nightmares. The incorporation of the ancient in the modern was a vision of history that continued to call for the methods of cultural history, and Warburg dedicated himself to building a library in which he would assemble the material for this vast project of cultural history. When Ernst Cassirer undertook his own cultural and philosophical examination of the origins of modernity in the late 1920s, he was strongly influenced by Aby Warburg, although his interpretation would go in such a different direction. Cassirer's research led him away from the Italy of ancient recollection and beautiful art, to a more northerly, more philosophical, and German context.

VIII. Crisis of Modernity
Cassirer

This was the complex state of historical understanding of the Renaissance, when the philosophers took up the question of the origins of
modernity in the early twentieth century. Ernst
Cassirer's approach to Nicholas of Cusa stemmed from his original research in the history of
philosophy, although he was aware of the fact
that in most historical accounts of the Renaissance, including Burckhardt's, Cusanus had no
part. Like historians of the Renaissance, Cassirer was aware of the forcefulness and inven-
tiveness of Petrarch's poetry, his familiar letters
and humanistic scholarship. The *Ascent of Mt.
Ventoux* allows us to observe the duality and
oscillation in the poet's understanding of nature and humanity. Petrarch "sees nature and
man, the world and history in a new splendor,"
but within a medieval framework of ideas.[115] It

---

[115] Cassirer, *Individual and Cosmos*, 144. Cassirer's
discovery of Cusanus and his earliest research in this
area is discussed in Morimichi Watanabe, "The Origins of Modern Cusanus Research in Germany and

was Nicholas of Cusa, however, whose way of thinking "stands at the narrow border between the times and between ways of thinking" connecting him to the emergence of the "new culture and the new humanity."[116]

Cassirer saw that *Kulturwissenschaft*, as practiced by Warburg, and embodied in his distinctive library, could support a new type of philosophical activity, and open a new scholarly horizon: the history of philosophy as cultural history.[117] This form of study would call for a combination of philosophical thought with a meticulous scholarly approach, "immersing itself in the most concrete particulars and in the most subtle nuances of historical detail."[118] In fineness of detail his methods of study departed from the sweeping style of *Geistesgeschichte* as practiced by contemporary historians, although he shared their interest in the connections between ideas and culture. For example,

---

the Establishment of the Heidelberg *Opera Omnia*," in Gerald Christianson and Thomas M. Izbicki, *Nicholas of Cusa in Search of God and Wisdom: Essays in Honor of Morimichi Watanabe*, Studies in the History of Christian Thought XLV (Leiden: E.J. Brill, 1991), 17–42, esp. 28–31.

[116] Cassirer, *Individual and Cosmos*, 37.

[117] Ferretti, *Cassirer, Panofsky, and Warburg*, 85. Ferretti makes Cassirer a neo-Kantian (as something unflattering), although contemporaries such as Edgar Wind, also affiliated with Warburg, recognized Cassirer's movement beyond neo-Kantianism to cultural history and a distinctive form of *Geistesgeschichte*. See Edgar Wind, "Contemporary German Philosophy," in *Journal of Philosophy* 22 (1925): 487–488 [477–493, 516–530].

[118] Cassirer, *Individual and Cosmos*, 5.

he appreciated the scholarship of Ernst Walser, and his vivid portrayal of the Renaissance as a complex period in which "the yearning for heaven and love of this earth are intertwined . . . in an infinitely . . . complex manner."[119] When Cassirer published his *Individual and Cosmos in Renaissance Philosophy*, as a volume in the *Studien der Bibliothek Warburg*, dedicating it to Aby Warburg, he hoped to balance and correct Burckhardt's lack of interest in philosophical factors in history.[120] Cassirer's reading of Burckhardt is evocative and positive.[121] While recognizing the significance of Burckhardt's thesis regarding the discovery of the individual, "that great process of liberation by which modern man matured towards a consciousness of himself," Cassirer disputed Burckhardt's understanding of the origins of the modern age.[122] Developments within German philosophy called for an explanation that would account for changes in cosmology and the structure of thought. For Cassirer, Nicholas of Cusa was the nonpareil of modernity.[123]

A distinctive feature of Cassirer's treatment of the Renaissance was the unanticipated em-

---

[119] Cassirer, *Individual and Cosmos*, 4–5. In this Cassirer was very close to the scholarly impulse of Aby Warburg.

[120] Original publication: Ernst Cassirer, *Individuum und Cosmos in der Philosophie der Renaissance*, Studien der Bibliothek Warburg 10 (Leipzig: Teubner, 1927).

[121] Cassirer, *Individual and Cosmos*, 86.

[122] Cassirer, *Individual and Cosmos*, 35.

[123] Schwartz, "Ernst Cassirer on Nicholas of Cusa," 26–27.

phasis on Nicholas of Cusa. Cassirer examined his thought as a departure from the other-worldliness of medieval theology and a radical turning toward the world. It seemed that Cusanus had attempted to join traditionally opposed concepts with his coincidence of opposites, by which he tried to reconcile divine transcendence and earthly particularity, thus to demonstrate the concord of God and man *in this world.* This would mean that the "The redemption of man . . . does not signify his liberation from a world worthy of being left behind because it is the inferior realm of the senses. Rather, redemption now applies to the whole of being."[124]

The *coincidentia oppositorum* was an important component of this intellectual liberation. In Cassirer's portrait, Nicholas of Cusa's life was filled with many obvious contradictions: he was plunged into the political affairs of his time, and yet as a contemplative, longed for a monk's cell in the Abbey of Tegernsee. His manner of thinking likewise contained oppositions: Cusanus ultimately came to believe that the "apex of theory" lay not in a distant region far from ordinary experience, but in the "very realm of empirical multiplicity; [that] indeed, [the height of philosophy] is a common, everyday matter."[125]

As Cassirer pointed out, Nicholas developed the insight that "the individual is not the

---

[124] Cassirer, *Individual and Cosmos*, 64. See further Cassirer's summary: "the universe is redeemed within man and through him" (40).

[125] Cassirer, *Individual and Cosmos*, 36.

opposite of the universal, but rather its true fulfillment." Individuality was itself a positive value. Cassirer noted the spiritual exercise, discussed earlier, of the *De visione Dei* with its establishment of the truth of the human face in the divine face. "In the cosmic order there is no absolute above and below, and . . . no body is closer or farther from the divine, original source of being than any other; rather, each is 'immediate to God'."[126] Each individual stands face to face with God. The reality of the individual is embraced only in the encounter with an all-seeing God. Therefore Cassirer contended that Cusa's doctrine of the human face, rather than his well-known scientific ideas, should be seen as the very focal point of his philosophy.[127] This conclusion is surprising, given Cassirer's own interest in science.

According to Cassirer, Cusa's doctrine of the human face, which prepared the way for modern individual existence, had its origins in his early education with the Brothers of the Common Life, and reflects the humanism and simplicity of the *devotio moderna*. This connection of Cusa's humanism to the modern devotion is no longer considered a significant source.[128] Secondly, Cusanus embraced the "spirit of Ger-

---

[126] The expression seems to contain an echo of Ranke. See Cassirer, *Individual and Cosmos*, 28.

[127] Cassirer, *Individual and Cosmos*, 33.

[128] Nicholas of Cusa did recognize this connection in a charitable sponsorship of poors students: see John Van Engen, *Sisters and Brothers of the Common Life: The Devotio Moderna and the World of the Later Middle Ages* (Philadelphia: University of Pennsylvania Press, 2008), 153.

man mysticism in all its speculative depth and in its moral and religious force."[129] As Cassirer noted, Nicholas was strongly influenced by Meister Eckhart. Thus a northern and German mystical element helped explain the philosophical profundity of Cusanus. The flowering of this as a new form of thought only came, however, with the additional lively influence of Italy and the embrace of antiquity underway at the University of Padua.[130]

Burckhardt had emphasized the emergence of modern human consciousness and self-awareness in the Italian Renaissance, as mankind awakened from a medieval slumber. The case of Cusanus showed instead that the discovery of "nature and man" emerged in the heart of the medieval world: "His greatness and his historical singularity consist in his having brought about this change not in opposition to the religious ideas of the Middle Ages, but from the standpoint of these ideas themselves."[131] In Cassirer's view, the strange imagery of the omnivoyant painting, the all-seeing face of God, allowed an authentic breakthrough for medieval theology and for the understanding and conceptualization of humanity.

Cassirer perhaps recognized in Cusanus someone who, like himself, confronted a world of political turbulence and great tension, for according to Cassirer: "[Nicholas] tried to embrace and to reconcile man and the cosmos,

---

[129] Cassirer, *Individual and Cosmos*, 33.

[130] Voigt, *Wiederbelebung des classischen Alterthums*, 1:441–442; Cassirer, *Individual and Cosmos*, 33.

[131] Cassirer, *Individual and Cosmos*, 36.

nature and history. But he underestimated the strength of the contending powers that were to be overcome and bound. This tragic error reveals itself not so much in his philosophy as in his life." Cassirer himself was determined to avoid that fate. Cassirer's study of Cusanus was published in the tense atmosphere following the Beer Hall Putsch of 1923. Cusanus, who lived and wrote during the collapse of *medieval civilization,* was therefore studied intensively again only in a later time of crisis, which threatened the collapse of *modern civilization.* The Weimar scholar and the Cardinal of Brixen called to one another from each end of the overarching structures of the modern world, as if from each end of a bridge.[132]

---

[132] The phenomenon seems to accord with Funkenstein's thesis of the response and echo of one period of crisis to an earlier: Amos Funkenstein, "Gershom Scholem: Charisma, *Kairos*, and the Messianic Dialectic," *History and Memory* 4 (1992): 123–140. See also Michael Edward Moore, "The Grace of Hermeneutics," *Glossator: Practice and Theory of the Commentary* 5 (2011): 163–172.

IX. Crisis of Modernity
Gadamer

Decades later, after the Second World War, Hans-Georg Gadamer also explored the importance of Cusanus in the history of philosophy and the transition from medieval to modern concepts.[133] In his principal work *Truth and Method* Gadamer marvelled at how Cusanus could break so decisively with medieval theories of language (as a fall from unity) and so decide instead that language and mental complexity were justified as a search for real correspondence with the world.[134] Cusanus helped to establish modern philosophy of language and hermeneutics as a general approach to knowledge about the world, and as such, Gadamer contended, should be seen as one of the

---

[133] Hans-Georg Gadamer, "Nicolaus von Cues und die Philosophie der Gegenwart," in Gadamer, *Kleine Schriften*, 5 vols. (Tübingen: J. Mohr/Siebeck, 1967-1972) 3:80–88.

[134] Gadamer, *Truth and Method*, 435.

great figures of western philosophical thought. In Nicholas of Cusa, language appears as a kind of light, flooding reality and making it visible.[135]

In 1964 the anniversary of the Cusan's death was marked by a conference in Padua on the theme 'Nicholas of Cusa as the beginning of the modern world,' at which Gadamer offered a paper.[136] His discussion begins with an historical account of how Cusanus came to have a position in European historical consciousness: this was "eine späte Entdeckung unserer geschichtlichen Bewußtseins."[137] Hegel had not known about Cusanus, nor had Schleiermacher. The interest in Cusanus emerged only slowly in the late nineteenth century: the first to take him up as a figure of philosophical importance had been the neo-Kantians, namely Otto Liebmann and

---

[135] Gadamer, *Truth and Method*, 503n11. Emmanuel Lévinas likewise spoke of language as something that moves through, and binds together, the world of light—i.e., the world in which we live, "un monde de transparence à travers lequel nous possédons le monde": Emmanuel Lévinas, *Parole et silence et autres conférences inédites au Collège* philosophique, eds. Rodolphe Calin and Catherine Chalier (Paris: Bernard Grasset, 2009), 90.

[136] Hans-Georg Gadamer, "Nikolaus von Kues im modernen Denken," in *Nicolo' Cusano agli inizi del mondo moderno*, Facoltà di Magistero dell' Università di Padova XII (Florence: G.C. Sansoni Editore, 1964), 39–48. Gadamer produced several closely related texts on this topic, one of which was translated into English by Theodore D. George: Hans-Georg Gadamer, "Nicolaus Cusanus and the Present," *Epoché* 7 (2002): 71–79.

[137] Gadamer, "Nikolaus von Kues," 39.

Hermann Cohen, the founder of the Marburg School. These thinkers were interested in Nicholas of Cusa because of his significance for the history of the natural sciences: providing the philosophical backdrop for Copernicus and Galileo.[138] Furthermore, "The Cusan taught that the quiddity of things, comprising their truth, is unreachable in its purity."[139] Because we cannot grasp reality directly, we can only rely on the appearances of things, *phantasmata*.[140] This construction goes back to Plato, but Nicholas accentuated it so strongly, in the view of Gadamer, that he tacitly becomes modern. It should be obvious why this concept would attract the notice of the neo-Kantian philosophers, as it seems to prepare the ground for the Kantian notion of the ungraspable *Ding-an-sich*.

According to Cusanus, the human spirit was made in the image of God and here we surely "stand at the origin of the entire essence of

---

[138] "Indem der Cusaner dieses platonische Motiv so entschieden akzentuiert, wird er auf eine ungewollte Weise, 'modern'": Gadamer, "Nikolaus von Kues," 40. Blumenberg denies Cusa any significant role in the development of a new cosmological schema: Blumenberg, *Legitimacy of the Modern Age*, 503, 510. Note that Blumenberg is also primarily interested in scientific thought, as an index of modernity, and in his view, Cusa's thought was no turning point.

[139] "Der Cusaner lehrt: die Quidditas der Dinge die ihre Wahrheit ausmacht ist in ihrer Reinheit unerreichbar": Gadamer, "Nikolaus von Kues," 41. On this point see also Vansteenberghe, *Cardinal Nicolas du Cues*, 381, who connects this teaching to Cusa's mysticism.

[140] Watts, *Nicolaus Cusanus*, 169.

modernity."[141] To illustrate this point, Gadamer
referred to the image of the Icon of God with
its distinctive presentation of the problem of
perspective, still a relatively new discovery in
the realm of painting. With this remarkable
image of an omnivoyant painting in mind, Cusanus could show that both the viewer and the
painting have a perspective of their own, and
this in turn helps to illustrate the correspondence of God and the individual. The human
perspective on God is as full of significance as
God's perspective on man. The ability to change
perspective, to see things from a different angle,
gives rise to the modern standpoint.

According to Gadamer, the thought of Cusanus was of the highest significance for certain
contemporary problems of philosophy arising
out of the researches of Old Testament scholars, such as Gogarten and Martin Buber, and
the hermeneutical problems they discovered
there, namely the *theology of the word*, later
radicalized by Heidegger. This was the very region of philosophy brought to a high degree of
intensity by Gadamer himself, a student of Heidegger and fascinated by problems of hermeneutics. As Buber and other Old Testament scholars agreed, the spirit and the world encounter
one another in the Word, in language. But the
humanism of Cusanus proved to be the significant element ushering in a modern standpoint. Cusanus often spoke of the human spirit as crea-

---

[141] "Hier stehen wir wirklich an einem Beginn des
ganzen neuzeitlichen Wesens": Gadamer, "Nikolaus
von Kues," 45. This doctrine, however, has earlier
medieval and patristic origins.

tive (*schöpferisch*).[142] God and humankind share this creative freedom.[143] This argument remains thoroughly theological and Christian, so we should not forget that "Cusan anthropology is Christology." Nevertheless, in Gadamer's view, we are here at the boundary of modernity, arising not out of cold hard advances of thought, but out of the pathos of a new feeling of life (*Lebensgefühl*)."[144]

Gadamer noted that while the neo-Kantians discovered Cusanus, the first important scholarly treatise was written only in 1927, by Ernst Cassirer. At that point, Cusanus entered the philosophical tradition and historical consciousness of Europe. Not long afterward, Raymond Klibansky and Ernst Hoffmann would initiate the critical edition of Nicholas of Cusa's collected works, under the auspices of the Heidelberg Academy of Sciences, published by Meiner Verlag.[145] As a result of Cassirer's fascination with this fifteenth-century Cardinal, his writings would be republished for the first time in 400 years.

---

[142] Gadamer, "Nikolaus von Kues," 43.

[143] "Gott und seiner Schöpfung wie in der schöpferischen Freiheit des Menschen das gleich ist": Gadamer, "Nikolaus von Kues," 48. Cassirer saw the recognition of human creativity and independence as a kind of liberation from the past achieved during the Renaissance: Baron, "Toward a More Positive Evaluation," 29.

[144] "So ist hier an der Schwelle der Neuzeit, aus dem Pathos des neuen Lebensgefühls heraus": Gadamer, "Nikolaus von Kues," 48.

[145] *Nicolai de Cusa Opera omnia iussu et auctoritate Acad- emiae Litterarum Heidelbergensis* (Hamburg, 1932-).

X. Crisis of Modernity
Blumenberg

The engagement of philosophy in cultural and hermeneutical questions led these thinkers to an involvement in historical problems. This was especially true in the development of modernity as a philosophical problem. For philosophy seemed to have gained its freedom only in the modern world: how had this come about? Nicholas of Cusa's life and writings were enacted, in the view of Hans Blumenberg, in the shadow of "the crisis-laden self-dissolution of the Middle Ages," a cultural collapse which threatened to destroy the centuries-old coherence of God, Man and the World.[146] According to Blumenberg, Nicholas deliberately endeavored to stop the disintegration of his world through his thought and writings. In contrast to the views of Cassirer and Gadamer, Nicholas of Cusa is for Blumenberg a figure who, in some sense, tried to stave off certain aspects of an emerging modernity.

As R. Wallace explains, Hans Blumenberg's

---

[146] Blumenberg, *Legitimacy of the Modern Age*, 484.

masterwork *The Legitimacy of the Modern Age* was intended as a rebuttal of the 1949 work of Karl Löwith, *Meaning in History*, a classic work that initiated a wide-ranging debate over the origins and character of modernity and historiography.[147] Löwith had maintained that the historical concepts of the Enlightenment and its faith in progress only echoed a much older tradition: modern history was dominated by the legacy of an age-old Jewish and Christian understanding of the nature of history.[148] Many of the most basic attitudes and concepts of modern understanding were secularized versions of older Christian ideas.[149] Time had a beginning and an end, and its meaning was constituted by the providential end toward which God was leading all things. The modern ideal of progress was nothing other than the secularization of Christian eschatology and its complementary historiography. Modernity itself was created out of old Jewish and Christian ingredients that were secularized, but remained mythic in struc-

---

[147] Robert M. Wallace, "Progress, Secularization and Modernity: The Löwith-Blumenberg Debate," *New German Critique* 22 (1981): 63–79. Wallace repeated this argument in his introduction to the 1983 translation of the *Legitimacy of the Modern Age.*

[148] "We of today, concerned with the unity of universal history and with its progress toward an ultimate goal . . . are still in the line of prophetic and messianic monotheism; we are still Jews and Christians": Karl Löwith, *Meaning in History* (Chicago: University of Chicago Press, 1949), 19.

[149] Elizabeth Brient, "Hans Blumenberg and Hannah Arendt on the 'Unworldly Worldliness' of the Modern Age," *Journal of the History of* Ideas 61 (2000): 517 [513–530].

ture and meaning.

Against Löwith, Hans Blumenberg argued that the modern age was something new and legitimate, a total break with the past.[150] While medieval Christianity had failed to resolve the Gnostic dilemma of the early Church, the modern age broke with the past and held out the possibility of a humanized world in which human beings could thrive.[151] This is Blumenberg's concept of worldliness, *Verweltlichung,* as humankind abandoned its long medieval experience of other-worldliness. He explicitly wrote *The Legitimacy of the Modern Age* as a response to Löwith, with the aim of vindicating certain notions such as enlightenment and progress as genuine concepts of a new age, the age of our own time. Nevertheless, it is no less certain that Jacob Burckhardt also cast a shadow over Blumenberg's project. Historical scholarship on the Renaissance and the origins of modernity entered Blumenberg's considerations as well as Löwith's philosophy of history.

In regard to the historical breakthrough at the heart of Blumbenberg's argument, Nicholas of Cusa appears as a solitary figure, seated on the medieval side of the boundary between the Middle Ages and Modernity. The static image of the Middle Ages served Blumenberg as a symbolic foil to recover the origins of moderni-

---

[150] With reference to Blumenberg's reaction to Löwith, see Hopkins, "Nicholas of Cusa," 29. See also Brient, "Hans Blumenberg and Hannah Arendt," 514–515.

[151] Michael Allen Gillespie, *The Theological Origins of Modernity* (Chicago: University of Chicago Press, 2008), 11.

ty in the late Renaissance, as a liberation from the medieval past: he clearly "proceeds from the assumption that human autonomy can henceforth articulate its positive character only outside the Middle Ages."[152] Nicholas was the last culminating figure of the medieval world, a thinker who tried to save the content and structure of the Middle Ages while combining it with a new craving for knowledge and new concepts.[153] Cusanus struggled in vain to "counteract the internal disintegration of the medieval system."[154]

Blumenberg conceptualized the appearance of modernity by reference to three key figures: Petrarch, Nicholas, and Giordano Bruno. Petrarch's *Ascent of Mont Ventoux* delights readers with its account of the poet's bold ascent to a new world, the moment when the Renaissance individual boldly turned his gaze toward nature, thereby "overstepping the limits" of the symbolically-encrusted medieval world. For Blumenberg this was not really a breakthrough: at the summit of Mont Ventoux, Petrarch turned back from the horizon of a new world to read a passage from Augustine's *Confessions*, retreating from the natural world, to turn his gaze inward.[155] "Then, happy to have seen enough of

[152] Blumenberg, *Legitimacy of the Modern Age*, 179.

[153] Blumenberg, *Legitimacy of the Modern Age*, 355.

[154] Blumenberg, *Legitimacy of the Modern Age*, 175.

[155] Blumenberg, *Legitimacy of the Modern Age*, 341–344. Blumenberg thereby rejected the central importance of Petrarch in Burckhardt and Voigt, and seems closer to Walser, for whom Petrarch was essentially similar to medieval scholars: Walser, *Gesammelte Studien*, 104.

the mountain, I turned my inner eye upon myself, and from that moment no one heard a
word from me until we reached the plain."[156]

At the other end of the epochal shift, according to Blumenberg, stood Giordano Bruno,
whose writings would become the true birth
certificate of modernity: here is the individual
striving to create and discover, the inquisitive
spirit that breaks decisively with the past.[157] But
here is something odd: for his knowledge of
Cusanus, Blumenberg relied on the nineteenth-
century Catholic historian F.J. Clemens. It is
quite unaccountable that he should not have
turned to the more recent and philosophically
profound work by Ernst Cassirer instead! Clemens perhaps had three sources of attraction
for Blumenberg: first, he was a Catholic author,
secondly he laid out the basic content and
character of Cusanus' thought, and thirdly, Clemens provided a German-philosophical vocabu-
lary in which he translated the unfamiliar concepts and terms of late medieval mentality.[158]
Clemens himself raised the great theme of Blumenberg's work, claiming that Nicholas was "a
gigantic spiritual presence at the end of the
Middle Ages and the beginning of the Modern."[159] The philosophy of Nicholas served as a

---

[156] Petrarch, *Familiares* 4.1, "To Dionigi da Borgo San
Sepolcro," translated in Peter Hainsworth, *The Essential Petrarch* (Indianapolis: Hackett, 2010), 225.

[157] Blumenberg, *Legitimacy of the Modern Age*, 524.

[158] Blumenberg, *Legitimacy of the Modern Age*, 479.
The work in question is F.J. Clemens, *Giordano Bruno und Nicolaus von Cusa. Eine philosophische Abhandlung* (Bonn: J. Wittmann, 1847).

[159] The possibilities of Blumenberg's analysis lie con-

hinge between two ages, lying precisely at the point of transformation, and yet not coming into focus: he was still wrapped in his medieval mantle of cloud. On the other hand, Nicholas was a master of the theory of numbers, of geometry, and could see into the structure of a decentered cosmos with amazing boldness.[160] According to Clemens, Cusanus thus introduced a liberated and non-mythic approach to nature.

Blumenberg interpreted the picture of God's face in Nicholas of Cusa's *De visione Dei* as an invitation to transform one's self-perception. In Cusa's "portrait that seems to look all of its viewers in the face at once," the humanistic consideration emerges, that all humans are seen directly by God, in such a way that there is no hierarchy, and all distinctions are leveled. "Thus each individual in his place stands immediately before the absolute."[161] While recognizing the theoretical advance and complexity in Cusa's image of the icon of God, Blumenberg sees it as ultimately a conservative and medieval conception.

Furthermore, according to Blumenberg, the metaphysical speculations of Cusanus contained no genuine presentiment of Copernican science. Here he dismissed his guide Clemens as unaccountably as he had taken him up: "this

---

tained here as if *in nuce*. "Wie eine geistige Riesengestalt am Schlusse der mittleren und am Eingange der neueren Zeit": Clemens, *Giordano Bruno und Nicolaus von Cusa*, 251.

[160] Clemens, *Giordano Bruno und Nicolaus von Cusa*, 97–102.

[161] Blumenberg, *Legitimacy of the Modern Age*, 538.

treatise from the middle of the nineteenth century is a piece of late Romanticism." [162] Blumenberg wants a resolutely *philosophical* account of modernism and his basic mode of
thought is hermeneutical. Therefore Nicholas
of Cusa must remain on the other side of the
"epochal threshold" between medieval and
modern, a boundary figure, a harbinger, a Mo-
ses on Mt. Pisgah who saw the modern but
could not attain it. [163] This view still contains
elements of the view maintained by Binz, who
was disappointed in the many signs of "ecclesiastical mysticism" to be found in the traditional
cleric Cusanus, who conformed to the procrus-
tean bed of the medieval world by accepting
the reality of witchcraft and by the restrictions
he imposed on the Jews of Germany. [164] Binz
was perhaps more clear-sighted on this issue
than many later scholars. [165]

Blumenberg was no historian. Blumenberg
never had recourse to the 1927 work of Ernst
Cassirer. His avoidance of Cassirer reflects a
well-known tendency to exclude this thinker
from the favored circle of Weimar era philosophers. "Ernst Cassirer, though by no means
entirely neglected, somehow seems too classi-
cally 'liberal,' too conventionally 'bourgeois' to

---

[162] Blumenberg, *Legitimacy of the Modern Age*, 479.

[163] On the concept of an epochal threshold, see Blumenberg, *Legitimacy of the Modern Age*, 478–479. In
this view, history does not move according to the
desire and action of individuals, or dateable events,
but moves through epochs, in a meaningful series of
effects.

[164] Binz, "Zur Charakteristik des Cusanus," 146.

[165] Vansteenberghe, *Cardinal Nicolas du Cues*, 138.

make his way into the current pantheon"—the pantheon of Weimar Jews who are most avidly studied and cited among contemporary academics. [166] Moreover, Blumenberg must have been aware of Cassirer's work. He consulted Rudolf Stadelmann's *Vom Geist des ausgehenden Mittelalters* of 1929, a gemlike study of late medieval Europe that places the work of Nicholas of Cusa in its historical and cultural context, "aus der spätmittelalterlichen Situation, nicht in der zeitlos abstrakten Luft der Doktrin gesehen."[167] As a cultural study of ideas this book was in tune with the approach of Cassirer, who is prominently cited therein. Blumenberg no doubt deliberately evaded Cassirer, whose basic thesis about Nicholas of Cusa would contradict his own.

Finally, Blumenberg reacted sharply against his former professor Gadamer, who had questioned his pupil's suggestion that Nicholas of Cusa was a figure of concern only in connection with the Middle Ages. In an early review of *The Legitimacy of the Modern Age*, Gadamer noted that Blumenberg had failed to understand Cusanus as someone who, with a sense of ease and lightness, "newly appropriates and transforms the entire heritage of Scholastic and ancient thought." [168] According to Gadamer,

---

[166] Steven E. Aschheim, *Beyond the Borders: The German-Jewish Legacy Abroad* (Princeton: Princeton University Press, 2007), 89–90.

[167] Stadelmann, *Vom Geist des ausgehenden Mittelalters*, 52. Stadelmann's approach is hermeneutical: "Historie ist Interpretation der Erscheinungen" (3).

[168] Karl Löwith and Hans-Georg Gadamer, "Hans Blu-

Blumenberg had to reject this idea, because it would undermine his thesis regarding the *epochal boundary* and the character of modernity. Blumenberg remarks that Cusanus was a prince of the Church whose attitude and sense of piety "is entirely rooted in the Middle Ages."[169] The question is a serious one, as Blumenberg notes, because it "promises to open up access to the problem of the legitimacy of the modern age."[170]

menberg: *Die Legitimät der Neuzeit,*" *Philosophische Rundschau* 15 (1968): 195–208. Cited in Blumenberg, *Legitimacy of the Modern Age,* 476.

[169] Blumenberg, *Legitimacy of the Modern Age,* 476.

[170] Blumenberg, *Legitimacy of the Modern Age,* 477.

XI. Mnemosyne and Modernity

When we examine the thought of Cusanus, with
its validation of historical humanity, we find that
this humanism contradicts other familiar notions about the meaning of modernity, such as
Max Weber's thesis of the progressive disenchantment of the world, in which the modernization of religion leads to a scientifically explained natural world, forcing humankind into
an unclouded confrontation with nature. [171]
Cusanus could only offer a modernity saturat-
ed in orthodox Christian themes. A special fascination attaches to Cusanus as one who lived
on the boundary between the medieval world
and the modern, as if he were seated at one
end of a bridge over a darkly flowing river. The
historian of philosophy Windelband aptly described Cusanus as a Janus-faced being who

---

[171] On the thesis of disenchantment, see Max Weber,
"Science as a Vocation," in *The Vocation Lectures*, ed.
David Owen and Tracy B. Strong, trans. Rodney Liv-
ingston (New York: Hackett, 2004), 13, 30.

looked back to the medieval past and forward to the modern.[172] It is true that Renaissance scholars and artists already sensed that they lived in a new era of history, and Nicholas himself was one of the first to make use of the historical concept of the Middle Ages.[173] The end of medieval political universalism, and the breaching of the strongholds of scholastic high culture by humanistic scholars are aspects of the *kairos* in which the concept of modernity was born, as a last age in which a dawn of truth might appear.

Historians and philosophers who attempt to understand modernity as a period of history rarely make clear which dimensions of modernity are in question, or what should count as modern. As we have seen, the historical face of Cusanus seems to look directly at every viewer, no matter which philosophical or historical questions are being asked of him, or which dimension of modernity is in question. This is a problem both of interpretation and of historical reminiscence, or to use Aby Warburg's terminology, *mnemosyne.*[174]

---

[172] Mentioned in Vansteenberghe, *Cardinal Nicolas du Cues*, 441. A similar point is made in Benoit Beyer de Ryke, "Nicolas de Cues, lecteur de Maître Eckhart," in *Nicolas de Cues, le méthodes d'une pensee* (Louvain-la-Neuve, 2005), 61 [61–77].

[173] On Renaissance views of historical change, see Hale, *Civilization of Europe*, 585–586. On Cusanus and the concept of a middle ages, see Paul Lehmann "Mittelalter und Küchenlatein," in *Erforschung des Mittelalters*, 53 [46–62]. See also Heussi, *Altertum, Mittelalter und Neuzeit*, 87.

[174] Mnemosyne was the motto of the Warburg Li-

Our sense of modernity is a response to that first crisis. The newfound promotion of the individual in Renaissance literature and art remains a significant landmark among the categories used by Jacob Burckhardt. In characterizing the shift from medieval to Renaissance, Joachim Leuschner later wrote: "the spiritual unrest of the late middle ages . . . brought about a process of individualization which in turn led to the emergence of what we tend to call modern man."[175] Modernity emerged out of spiritual unrest and disquiet: but might it not be said that modernity is a term for a certain unrest and disquiet? A sense of disquiet colors the spiritual gains that might come with a modern stance.

Hans Ulrich Gumbrecht showed that writers of the Middle Ages already used the expression *modern,* to indicate any rejection of good old tradition.[176] In religious life, the term *devotio moderna* referred to groups practicing a new style of spirituality in northern Europe during the later Middle Ages, the tradition in

---

brary. The concept of reminiscence and archaeology of culture as used by Warburg can be compared to the problematics of cultural history in the Hegelian tradition: Ernst Cassirer, *Symbol, Myth, and Culture,* ed. Donald Phillip Verene (New Haven: Yale University Press, 1979), 78–79.

[175] Leuschner, *Germany in the Late Middle Ages,* xxix.

[176] Hans Ulrich Gumbrecht, "Modern, Modernität, Moderne," in *Geschichtliche Grundbegriffe. Historisches Lexikon zur politisch-sozialen Sprache in Deutschland,* eds. Otto Brunner, Werner Conze, and Reinhart Koselleck, 8 vols.-in-9 (Stuttgart: E. Klett, 1972-1997), 4:93–131.

which Nicholas of Cusa had his childhood education. This devotion was "modern" in the sense that it attempted to practice piety in the present age, to search for spiritual *presence*. The spirituality of the movement was deeply traditional and in many ways medieval, even though it was a response to disquiet, a harbinger of religious modernity and the Reformation. [177] The humanists discovered the keys of modernity in the soil of the ancient past.

While the modern era may have begun in the Renaissance, after World War One a gulf opened between the modern world and the past. [178] A melancholy love of the beautiful in nature no longer underpinned the modern consciousness, nor did an appreciation of ancient literature. We lost our connection to the ideals of the Renaissance and the scholarly practices of humanism. [179] Thus western-oriented thought seemed

---

[177] Discussion of the term and historiography in John van Engen, *Sisters and Brothers of the Common Life*, 1–10. Regarding the connection between modernity and restorations of the past, see Otto Gründler, "*Devotio moderna atque antiqua*: The Modern Devotion and Carthusian Spirituality," in *The Roots of the Modern Christian Tradition*, ed. E. Rozanne Elder (Kalamazoo: Cistercian Publications, 1984) [= *The Spirituality of Western Christendom* II], 27–45.

[178] "America, in a sense, was that gulf." American culture has a certain claim to epitomise modernity, according to a profound and delightful essay by Edmund Wilson: "A Preface to Persius: Maudlin Meditations in a Speakeasy," in Edmund Wilson, *The Shores of Light: A Literary Chronicle of the 1920s and 1930s* (New York: Noonday Press, 1952), 273 [267–273].

[179] Burdach, *Reformation, Renaissance, Humanismus*, 178.

to enter unfamiliar country.

Koselleck rightly remarks that, "our concept of modernity (*Neuzeit*) is . . . enormously elastic. An early modern period has been distinguished from modernity in a strict sense," while the boundaries between eras have been reimagined as "epochal thresholds" or periods of transition.[180] With the concept of *modernity* we might be seeking the origin of our industrial and technocratic world, and the sources of our alienation, as Földényi would have it.[181] Hegel described modernity as our alienated existence on a de-mythologized planet, deprived of the intensity of life, and the joy that once stemmed from ordinary human activities.[182] In the view of Hannah Arendt, the transition amounts to the loss of the world, *Entweltlichung*.[183]

European philosophers have tended to focus on this dimension. Jan Patocka, glossing Husserl, saw in modernity a teleological princi-

---

[180] Reinhart Koselleck, "The Eighteenth Century as the Beginning of Modernity," in: *The Practice of Conceptual History: Timing History, Spacing Concepts* (Stanford: Stanford University Press, 2002), 155 [154–169].

[181] "La technique est le véritable vainqueur du XXe siècle. Le moyen 'athée,' c'est-à-dire terrestre, est devenu une 'fin divine,' une transcendance exclusive: elle a aliéné l'homme de lui-même": László F. Földényi, *Dostoïevski lit Hegel en Sibérie et fond en larmes*, trans. Natalia Zaremba-Huzsvai and Charles Zaremba (Arles: Actes Sud, 2008), 51.

[182] Michael N. Forster, *Hegel's Idea of a Phenomenology of Spirit* (Chicago: University of Chicago Press, 1998), 61–63.

[183] Brient, "Hans Blumenberg and Hannah Arendt," 515.

ple, which presupposes that former times and events culminated in western technology and rationality. Thus modernity "distinguishes European culture above all others."[184] But there are many possible shades of meaning, and many losses to tally, when scholars try to account for the "intolerable fragmentation" of modern times.[185] Later critics have seen modernity as leading inevitably to the barbarism and massacres of World War Two. In Zygmunt Bauman's analysis, we are left with a "gnawing suspicion" that humanity has "melted all that was solid and profaned all that was sacred."[186] According to the theologian Hans Urs von Balthasar, "what we call our culture flees blindly from the meaninglessness which surrounds us on all sides." An empty desert of alienation, *regio dissimilitudinis*, must serve as the setting for ascetic experience, just as the desert served the hermits and monks of old. Loss of meaning in the

---

[184] Jan Patocka, *Heretical Essays in the Philosophy of History*, trans. Erazim Kohák (Chicago: Open Court, 1996), 44.

[185] Scott Spector, *Prague Territories: National Conflict and Cultural Innovation in Frankz Kafka's Fin de Siècle* (Berkeley: University of California Press, 2000), 35. See also Carol Symes, "When We Talk about Modernity," *The American Historical Review* 116 (2011): 715–726. The problemata of the concept *modernity* equally cast doubt on the concept of the *Middle Ages*. Symes's paper was part of a roundtable that revealed the multiplicity of possible connotations for modernity, and the association of this concept with favored historiographical positions.

[186] Zygmunt Bauman, "Modernity and Clarity: The Story of a Failed Romance," in *The Individualized Society* (Cambridge, Eng.: Polity, 2001), 58 [57–70].

modern *saeculum* reflects a desertification of the world, from the concentration camp to the cancer ward.[187] This portrait of an empty world would direct our gaze to a confrontation with the divine in which the world begins to lose its hold on us.

Nicholas of Cusa tried to renovate the world of his time with all its grievous conflicts, and faced a philosophical tradition bitterly divided between two tendencies. His dilemma seemed painfully familiar to Ernst Cassirer. I have suggested that the *kairos* of 1453 corresponded to the *kairos* of 1923-1933. In the work of Nicholas of Cusa, Cassirer explained, "Philosophy becomes the defensive bulwark against worldly forces pressing from all sides."[188] In later essays Cassirer condemned Martin Heidegger for violating that very principle, and indeed, when the crisis arrived, Heidegger turned out to be on the side of 'worldly forces.'[189] The later philosophical conflict made visible the thorny barriers between Cassirer, the Jewish liberal, and Blumenberg, the Catholic convert. Likewise, we have noted a conflict between

---

[187] Hans Urs von Balthasar, *Elucidations*, trans. John Riches (San Francisco: Ignatius Press, 1998), 61, 203–203, and *Christian Meditation*, trans. Sister Mary Theresilde Skerry (San Francisco: Ignatius Press, 1989), 70.

[188] Cassirer, *Individual and Cosmos*, 61.

[189] "A philosophy that indulges in somber predictions about the decline and the inevitable destruction of human culture, a philosophy whose whole attention is focused on the *Geworfenheit*, the Being-thrown of man, can no longer do its duty": Cassirer, *Symbol, Myth, and Culture*, 230.

Blumenberg and his teacher, Gadamer. Gadamer remained a faithful student of Heidegger but appreciated Cassirer's historical research and its philosophical purpose, which brought Nicholas of Cusa into the historical and philosophical consciousness of Europe. We can also point to Cassirer's desire to defend human culture and the possibility of a common world against dire threats of fascism and racism. All of these conflicts came into focus around the complex legacy of Nicholas of Cusa.

If modernity is a messianic concept of time, open to an unknown future, then our connection to the present must be restrained. Perhaps we are only sojourning here, poised and waiting for the end of time.[190] On the other hand, just as urgently as during the Renaissance, it would seem that the "heart of modernity" is open to the "heart of antiquity." The capacity of ruins to communicate, and the interest of ancient writings might be marvelled at again. Nicholas of Cusa demonstrated that a return to antiquity could lead to the discovery of new paths during a historical period of spiritual disquiet and political crisis. This included a scholarly openness to Islam and its adherents, and possible solutions to difficult constitutional problems such as the Great Schism.

In 1932, another Jewish scholar interested in Nicholas of Cusa, Raymond Klibansky, a close associate of Cassirer, helped to initiate the Heidelberg Academy edition of the works of

---

[190] On the concept of sojourning in messianic time, see Giorgio Agamben, *The Church and the Kingdom*, trans. Leland de la Durantaye (London: Seagull, 2012), 2.

Nicholas of Cusa, mentioned earlier.[191] Then in 1933, just days before Hitler's control over German cultural life was completely established, Klibansky helped Fritz Saxl to spirit away the Warburg Library by packing its 100, 000 volumes and quietly shipping them to England aboard two steamships sailing from Hamburg. Thus an incomparable instrument for the study of the passage of human consciousness from antiquity to modern times was preserved, and is housed at the University of London. In 1933, Cassirer left his post in Hamburg and also went to England. Years later, at the end of World War Two, it was said, Klibansky, who worked for British intelligence, was able to convince the British air command to spare Kues, the birthplace of Nicholas, from the allied bombing campaign. Thereby were saved the medieval hospital Nicholas had founded for the support of the elderly, the treasures of his humanistic library, and the brass tablet where his heart lies buried.

---

[191] Watanabe offers some remarks on Klibansky's understanding of Nicholas of Cusa, and some useful signposts: Watanabe, "Origins of Modern Cusanus Research," 33–34.

References

𝄢

I. Works of Nicholas of Cusa

Haec Accurata Recognitio Trium Voluminum Operum Clariss. P. Nicolai Cusae Card. Ex Officina Ascensiana Recenter Emissa Est, ed. Jacques Lèfevre d'Etaples. Josse Badius, 1514. [Wolfenbüttel: Herzog August Bibliothek, H: P 556.2° Helmst. (1)].

Nicholas of Cusa. *La Vision de Dieu par le Cardinal Nicolas de Cuse (1401-1464)*, trans. Edmond Vansteenberghe. Louvain: Éditions de Museum Lessianum, 1925.

Nicolai de Cusa Opera omnia iussu et auctoritate Academiae Litterarum Heidelbergensis. Hamburg: In Aedibus Felicis Meiner, 1932-. [=Nicholas of Cusa. *Opera Omnia*].

Nicholas of Cusa. *Opera Omnia*, vol. XII: *De venatione sapientiae; De apice theoriae,* eds. R. Klibansky and H(ans). G. Senger. Hamburg: In Aedibus Felicis Meiner, 1981.

Nicholas of Cusa. *The Catholic Concordance*, trans. Paul E. Sigmund. Cambridge, Eng.: Cambridge University Press, 1991.

Nicholas of Cusa. *Opera Omnia,* vol. VI: *De Visione Dei*, ed. Adelaida Dorothea Riemann. Hamburg: In

Aedibus Felicis Meiner, 2000.

Complete Philosophical and Theological Treatises of Nicholas of Cusa, trans. Jasper Hopkins. 2 vols. Minneapolis: J. Banning Press, 2001.

II. Treatises about Nicholas

Albertini, Tamara. "Mathematics and Astronomy." In Bellitto et al., *Introducing Nicholas of Cusa*, 373–406.

Bellitto, Christopher M., Thomas M. Izbicki, and Gerald Christianson, eds. *Introducing Nicholas of Cusa: A Guide to a Renaissance Man*. New York: Paulist Press, 2004.

Beyer de Ryke, Benoit. "Nicolas de Cues, lecteur de Maître Eckhart." In *Nicolas de Cues, les méthodes d'une pensée. Actes du Colloque de Louvain-la-Neuve*, eds. Jean-Michel Counet and Stéphane Mercier, 61–77. Louvain-la-Neuve: Collège Érasme, 2005.

Biechler, James E. "Interreligious Dialogue," in Bellitto at al., eds., *Introducing Nicholas of Cusa*, 270–296.

Binz, Carl. "Zur Charakteristik des Cusanus," *Archiv für Kulturgeschichte* 7 (1909): 145–153.

Bond, H. Lawrence. "The 'Icon' and the 'Iconic Text.' In *Nicholas of Cusa and his Age: Intellect and Spirituality: Essays Dedicated to the Memory of F. Edward Cranz, Thomas P. McTighe and Charles Trinkaus*, ed. Thomas M. Izbicki, 177–197. Studies in the History of Christian Thought 105. Leiden: Brill, 2002.

Buber, Martin. "On the History of the Problem of Individuation: Nicholas of Cusa and Jakob Böhme," trans. Sarah Scott. *Graduate Faculty Philosophy Journal* 33 (2012): 371–401.

Buber, Martin. *Zur Geschichte des Individuationsproblems. Nicolaus von Cues und Jakob Böhme*. PhD diss. University of Vienna, 1904.

Cassirer, Ernst. *Individual and Cosmos in Renaissance Philosophy*, trans. Mario Domandi. Oxford: Basil Blackwell, 1963.

Cassirer, Ernst. *Individuum und Cosmos in der Philosophie der Renaissance*. Studien der Bibliothek Warburg 10. Leipzig: Teubner, 1927.

Certeau, Michel de. "The Gaze: Nicholas of Cusa." *Diacritics* 17 (1987): 2–38.

Clemens, F. J. *Giordano Bruno und Nicolaus von Cusa. Eine philosophische Abhandlung*. Bonn: J. Wittmann, 1847.

Duclow, Donald F. "Life and Works." In Bellitto et al., *Introducing Nicholas of Cusa*, 29–56.

Duhem, Pierre. "Nicolas de Cues et Léonard de Vinci." *Bulletin Italien* VII (1907) 87–134, 181–220, 314–329; and VIII (1908): 18–55, 116–147.

Dzieduszycki, Adalbert Graf. "Die Philosophie des Kardinals Nicolaus von Kusa." *Die Kultur* 5 (1904): 24–61.

Flasch, Kurt. *Nikolaus von Kues. Geschichte einer Entwicklung. Vorlesunen zur Einführung in seine Philosophie*. Frankfurt-am-Main: Vittorio Klostermann, 1998.

Gadamer, Hans-Georg. "Nicolaus Cusanus and the Present," trans. Theodore D. George, *Epoché* 7 (2002): 71–79.

Gadamer, Hans-Georg. "Nicolaus von Cues und die Philosophie der Gegenwart." In Hans-Georg Gadamer, *Kleine Schriften*. 5 vols. Tübingen: J. Mohr/Siebeck, 1967-1972. 3:80–88.

Gadamer, Hans-Georg. "Nikolaus von Kues im modernen Denken." In *Nicolo' Cusano agli inizi del mondo moderno*, 39–48. Facoltà di Magistero dell' Università di Padova XII. Florence: G. C. Sansoni Editore, 1964.

Haas, Alois Maria. *Deum mistice videre...in caligine coincidencie. Zum Verhältnis Nicolaus' von Kues zur Mystik*. Vorträge der Aeneas-Silvius-Stiftung an der Universität Basel XXIV. Basel: Verlag Halbing & Lichtenhahn, 1989.

Hopkins, Jasper. "Nicholas of Cusa (1401-1464): First Modern Philosopher?" *Midwest Studies in Philosophy* 16 (2002): 13–29.

Magnard, Paul. "La chasse de la sagesse: Une topique de l'oeuvre du Cusain." In Counet and Mercier, *Nicolas de Cues*, 79–87.

Müller, Tom. *"Ut reiecto paschali errore veritati insistamus": Nikolaus von Kues und seine Konzilsschrift* De reparatione kalendarii. Münster: Aschendorff Verlag, 2010.

Nicolas de Cues, les méthodes d'une pensée. Actes du Colloque de Louvain-la-Neuve, eds. Jean-Michel Counet and Stéphane Mercier. Louvain-la-Neuve: Collège Érasme, 2005.

Saitta, Giuseppe. *Nicolò Cusano e l'umanisimo italiano.* Bologna: Tamari Editori, 1957.

Schwartz, Yossef. "Ernst Cassirer on Nicholas of Cusa: Between Conjectural Knowledge and Religious Pluralism." In Jeffrey Andrew Barash, *The Symbolic Construction of Reality: The Legacy of Ernst Cassirer,* 17–39. Chicago: University of Chicago Press, 2008.

Trottmann, Christian. "La docte ignorance dans le *De Icona*. L'humanisme de l'au dela du concept." In Counet and Mercier, *Nicolas de Cues,* 105–116.

Vansteenberghe, Edmond. *Le Cardinal Nicolas du Cues (1401-1464). L'Action—la pensée.* Paris: Honoré Champion, 1920.

Watanabe, Morimichi. "Nicolaus Cusanus, Monastic Reform in the Tyrol and the *De Visione Dei.*" In *Concordia discors. Studi su Niccolò Cusano e l'umanesimo europeo offerti a Giovanni Santinello,* ed. Gregorio Piaia, 181–197. Padua: Editrice Antenore, 1993.

Watanabe, Morimichi. "The Origins of Modern Cusanus Research in Germany and the Establishment of the Heidelberg *Opera Omnia*." In *Nicholas of Cusa in Search of God and Wisdom: Essays in Honor of Morimichi Watanabe*, eds. Gerald Christianson and Thomas M. Izbicki, 17–42. Studies in the History of Christian Thought XLV. Leiden: E.J. Brill, 1991.

Watanabe, Morimichi. *The Political Ideas of Nicholas of Cusa, with Special Reference to his* De Concordantia catholica. Geneva: Librairie Droz, 1963.

Watts, Pauline Moffit. *Nicolaus Cusanus: A Fifteenth-Century Vision of Man*. Studies in the History of Christian Thought XXX. Leiden: E.J. Brill, 1982.

Zellinger, Eduard. *Cusanus-Konkordanz. Unter Zugrundelegung der philosophischen und der bedeutendsten theologischen Werke*. Munich: Max Heuber Verlag, 1960.

III. Historiography & Theory

Agamben, Giorgio. *The Church and the Kingdom*, trans. Leland de la Durantaye. London: Seagull, 2012.

Aschheim, Steven E. *Beyond the Borders: The German-Jewish Legacy Abroad*. Princeton: Princeton University Press, 2007.

Aubens, Roger, and Robert Ricard. *L'Église et la Renaissance (1449-1517)*. Paris: Bloud & Gay, 1951. [=Augustin Fliche and Victor Martin, eds. *Histoire de l'Église depuis les origines jusqu'a nos jours*, Vol. 15].

Baron, Hans. "Toward a More Positive Evaluation of the Fifteenth-Century Renaissance." *Journal of the History of Ideas* 4 (1943): 21–49.

Bauman, Zygmunt. *The Individualized Society*. Cambridge, Eng.: Polity, 2001.

Becker, Marvin B. *Civility and Society in Western Europe, 1300-1600*. Bloomington: Indiana University, 1988.

Beiser, Frederick. *Hegel.* New York: Routledge, 2005.

Blumenberg, Hans. *The Legitimacy of the Modern Age,* trans. Robert M. Wallace. Cambridge, Mass.: MIT Press, 1983.

Blumenberg, Hans. *Shipwreck with Spectator: Paradigm of a Metaphor for Existence,* trans. Steven Rendall. Cambridge, Mass.: MIT Press, 1997.

Borchardt, Frank L. *German Antiquity in Renaissance Myth.* Baltimore: Johns Hopkins University Press, 1971.

Boudet, Jacques. *Les Mots de l'histoire.* Paris: Robert Laffont, 1990.

Bouyer, Louis. *Autour d'Erasme.* Paris: Cerf, 1955.

Brooks, Van Wyck. *The Dream of Arcadia: American Artists and Writers in Italy, 1760-1915.* New York: Dutton, 1958.

Burckhardt, Jacob. *Reflections on History.* Indianapolis: Liberty Classics, 1979.

Burckhardt, Jacob. *The Civilization of the Renaissance in Italy.* 3d edn. London: Phaidon, 2006.

Burdach, Konrad. *Reformation, Renaissance, Humanismus: Zwei Abhandlungen über die Grundlage moderner Bildung und Sprachkunst.* Berlin: Gebrüder Paetel, 1918.

Bursian, Conrad. *Geschichte der classischen Philologie in Deutschland von den Anfängen bis zur Gegenwart.* Munich: R. Oldenbourg, 1883.

Cassirer, Ernst. *Symbol, Myth, and Culture,* ed. Donald Phillip Verene. New Haven: Yale University Press, 1979.

Chiffoleau, Jacques. *La religion flamboyante. France, 1320-1520.* Paris: Éditions Points, 2011.

Conway, David. "A Head of Christ by John Van Eyck." *The Burlington Magazine 39* (1921): 253–255, 257, 260.

Ferguson, Wallace K.. *The Renaissance in Historical Thought: Five Centuries of Interpretation.* Cambridge, Eng.: Riverside Press, 1948.

Ferretti, Silvia. *Cassirer, Panofsky, and Warburg: Symbol, Art and History.* New Haven: Yale University Press, 1989.

Földényi, László F. *Dostoïevski lit Hegel en Sibérie et fond en larmes,* trans. Natalia Zaremba-Huzsvai and Charles Zaremba. Arles: Actes Sud, 2008.

Forster, Michael N. *Hegel's Idea of a Phenomenology of Spirit.* Chicago: University of Chicago Press, 1998.

Funkenstein, Amos. "Gershom Scholem: Charisma, *Kairos,* and the Messianic Dialectic." *History and Memory* 4 (1992): 123–140.

Gadamer, Hans-Georg. *Truth and Method,* trans. Joel Weinsheimer and Donald G. Marshall. 2d edn. New York: Continuum, 1998.

Garner, Roberta. "Jacob Burckhardt as a Theorist of Modernity: Reading *The Civilization of the Renaissance in Italy.*" *Sociological Theory* 8 (1990): 48–57.

Gebhart, Émile. *Les origines de la Renaissance en Italie.* Paris: Hachette, 1879.

Gilbert, Felix. "Jacob Burckhardt's Student Years: The Road to Cultural History." *Journal of the History of Ideas* 47 (1986): 249–274.

Gillespie, Michael Allen. *The Theological Origins of Modernity.* Chicago: University of Chicago Press, 2008.

Gordon, Peter Eli. *Continental Divide: Heidegger, Cassirer, Davos.* Cambridge, Mass.: Harvard University Press, 2010.

Gossman, Lionel. *Basel in the Age of Burckhardt: An Age of Unseasonable Ideas.* Chicago: University of Chicago Press, 2000.

Greenblatt, Stephen. *The Swerve: How the World Became Modern.* New York: W.W. Norton, 2011.

Gründler, Otto. "*Devotio moderna atque antiqua:* The Modern Devotion and Carthusian Spirituality." In *The Roots of the Modern Christian Tradition,* ed. E. Rozanne Elder, 27–45. The Spirituality of Western

Christendom II. Kalamazoo: Cistercian Publications, 1984.

Gumbrecht, Hans Ulrich. "Modern, Modernität, Moderne." In *Geschichtliche Grundbegriffe. Historisches Lexikon zur politisch-sozialen Sprache in Deutschland*, eds. Otto Brunner, Werner Conze, and Reinhart Koselleck. 8 vols.-in-9. Stuttgart: E. Klett, 1972-1997. 4:93–131.

Hadot, Pierre. *What is Ancient Philosophy*, trans. Michael Chase. Cambridge, Mass.: Belknap Press, 2001.

Hale, John. *The Civilization of Europe in the Renaissance*. New York: Athenaeum, 1994.

Hay, Denys. *Europe in the Fourteenth and Fifteenth Centuries*. 2d edn. London: Longman, 1989.

Heer, Friedrich. *The Intellectual History of Europe*, trans. Jonathan Steinberg. Cleveland: World Publishing Co., 1966.

Heussi, Karl. *Altertum, Mittelalter und Neuzeit in der Kirchengeschichte; ein Beitrag zum Problem der historischen Periodisierung*. 1921; repr. Darmstadt: Wissenschaftliche Buchgesellschaft, 1969.

Hinde, John R. *Jacob Burckhardt and the Crisis of Modernity*. Montreal: McGill-Queen's University Press, 2000.

Hölderlin, Friedrich. *Poems and Fragments*, trans. Michael Hamburger. London: Anvil Press Poetry, 2004.

Hollier, Denis. *A New History of French Literature*. Cambridge, Mass.: Harvard University Press, 1989.

Huizinga, Johann. *The Autumn of the Middle Ages*, trans. Rodney J. Payton and Ulrich Mammitzsch. Chicago: University of Chicago Press, 1996.

Janssen, Jean. *L'Allemagne à la fin du Moyen Âge*. Paris: E. Plon, Nourrit et Cie., 1887.

Janssen, Johannes. *Geschichte des deutschen Volkes seit dem Ausgang des Mittelalters*. 8 vols. Freiburg im Breisgau: Herder, 1879-1894.

Judet de la Combe, Pierre. "Classical Philology and the

Making of Modernity in Germany." In *Multiple Antiquities—Multiple Modernities: Ancient Histories in Nineteenth Century European Cultures*, eds. Gábor Klaniczay, Michael Werner, and Ottó Gecser, 65–88. Frankfurt: Campus Verlag, 2011.

Koselleck, Reinhart. *The Practice of Conceptual History: Timing History, Spacing Concepts*, trans. Todd Samuel Presner. Stanford: Stanford University Press, 2002.

Koyré, Alexandre. *The Astronomical Revolution, Copernicus—Kepler—Borelli*, trans. R.E.W. Maddison. Ithaca: Cornell University Press, 1973.

Kristeller, Paul Oskar. "Humanism and Scholasticism in the Italian Renaissance." In Kristeller, *Renaissance Thought and its Sources*, 85–105.

Kristeller, Paul Oskar. "Renaissance Philosophy and the Medieval Tradition." In Kristeller, *Renaissance Thought and its Sources*, 106–133.

Kristeller, Paul Oskar. *Renaissance Thought and its Sources*, ed. Michael Mooney. New York: Columbia University Press, 1979.

Lehmann, Paul. *Erforschung des Mittelalters. Ausgewählte Abhandlungen und Aufsätze.* 5 vols. Stuttgart: Anton Hiersemann, 1959-1962.

Lehmann, Paul. "Grundzüge des Humanismus deutscher Lande zumal im Spiegel deutscher Bibliotheken des 15. 16. Jahrhunderts." In Lehmann, *Erforschung des Mittelalters*, 5:481–496.

Lehmann, Paul. "Mittelalter und Küchenlatein." In Lehmann, *Erforschung des Mittelalters*, 1:46–62.

Lehmann, Paul. "The Benedictine Order and the Transmission of the Literature of Ancient Rome in the Middle Ages." In Lehmann, *Erforschung des Mittelalters*, 3:173–183.

Leuschner, Joachim. *Germany in the Late Middle Ages*, trans. Sabine MacCormack. Amsterdam: North-Holland Publishing, 1980.

Levinas, Emmanuel. *Humanism of the Other*, trans.

Richard A. Cohen. Urbana: University of Illinois Press, 2003.

Lévinas, Emmanuel. *Parole et silence et autres conférences inédites au Collège philosophique*, eds. Rodolphe Calin and Catherine Chalier. Paris: Bernard Grasset, 2009.

Liebeschütz, Hans. "Aby Warburg (1866-1929) as Interpreter of Civilisation." *Leo Baeck Institute Yearbook* XVI (1971): 225–236.

Löwith, Karl and Hans-Georg Gadamer. "Hans Blumenberg: *Die Legitimät der Neuzeit*." *Philosophische Rundschau* 15 (1968): 195–208.

Löwith, Karl. *Martin Heidegger and European Nihilism*, trans. Gary Steiner. New York: Columbia University Press, 1995.

Löwith, Karl. *Meaning in History*. Chicago: University of Chicago Press, 1949.

Mazzotta, Giuseppe. *The Worlds of Petrarch*. Durham: Duke University Press, 1993.

Michelet, Jules. *Renaissance*. Paris: Chamerot, 1855.

Modernism, 1890-1930, eds. Malcolm Bradbury and James McFarlane. Penguin: Harmondsworth, 1976.

Moore, Michael Edward. "Meditations on the Face in the Middle Ages (With Levinas and Picard)." *Literature and Theology* 24 (2010): 19–37.

Moore, Michael Edward. "The Grace of Hermeneutics." *Glossator: Practice and Theory of the Commentary* 5 (2011): 163–172.

Neumann, Carl. "Ranke und Burckhardt und die Geltung des Begriffes 'Renaissance' insbesondere für Deutschland." *Historische Zeitschrift* 150 (1934): 485–496.

Nolhac, Pierre de. *Petrarque et l'humanisme d'après un essai de restitution de sa bibliothèque*. Paris: É. Bouillon, 1892.

Nolhac, Pierre de. *Petrarque et l'humanisme*. 2 vols. 2d edn. Paris: Honoré Champion, 1907.

Nordström, Johan. *Moyen Âge et Renaissance. Essai*

historique, trans. T. Hammar. Paris: Librairie Stock, 1933.

Oberman, Heiko A.. *The Dawn of the Reformation: Essays in Late Medieval and Early Reformation Thought.* Grand Rapids: Eerdmans Publishing, 1986.

Panofsky, Erwin. *"Facies illa Rogeri maximi pictoris."* In *Late Classical and Mediaeval Studies in Honor of Albert Mathias Friend,* ed. Kurt Weitzmann, 392–400. Princeton: Princeton University Press, 1955.

Panofsky, Erwin. "Reflections on Historical Time," trans. Johanna Baumann. *Critical Inquiry* 30 (2004): 691–701.

Patocka, Jan. *Heretical Essays in the Philosophy of History,* trans. Erazim Kohák. Chicago: Open Court, 1996.

Petrarch, Francesco. *The Essential Petrarch,* trans. Peter Hainsworth. Indianapolis: Hackett, 2010.

Philippides, Marios and Walter K. Hanak. *The Siege and Fall of Constantinople in 1453: Historiography, Topography, and Military Studies.* Surrey: Ashgate, 2011.

Ritter, Joachim, and Karlfried Gründer. *Historisches Wörterbuch der Philosophie.* Darmstadt: Wissenschaftliches Buchgesellschaft, 1984.

Roeck, Berndt. *Florence 1900: The Quest for Arcadia,* trans. Stuart Spencer. New Haven: Yale University Press, 2009.

Schapiro Meyer. *Words and Pictures: On the Literal and the Symbolic in the Illustration of a Text.* The Hague: Mouton, 1973.

Settis, Salvatore. *The Future of the "Classical,"* trans. Allan Cameron. Cambridge, Eng.: Polity Press, 2006.

Sonkes, Micheline. *Dessins du XVe siècle: Groupe van der Weyden, Essai de catalogue des originaux du maître, des copies et des dessins anonymes inspireés par son style.* Brussels: Centre National de Recherches, 1969.

Spector, Scott. *Prague Territories: National Conflict and Cultural Innovation in Frankz Kafka's Fin de Siècle.* Berkeley: University of California Press, 2000.

Spitz, Lewis W. "Reflections on Early and Late Humanism: Burckhardt's Morality and Religion." In *Jacob Burckhardt and the Renaissance 100 Years After,* 15–27. Lawrence: University of Kansas Museum of Art, 1960.

Stadelmann, Rudolf. *Vom Geist des ausgehenden Mittelalters.* 1929; repr. Stuttgart: Friedrich Frommann Verlag [Günther Holzboog], 1966.

Swiezawski, Stefan. *Histoire de la philosophie européenne au XVe siècle.* Paris: Beauchesne, 1990.

Symes, Carol. "When We Talk about Modernity." *The American Historical Review* 116 (2011): 715–726.

Van Engen, John. *Sisters and Brothers of the Common Life: The Devotio Moderna and the World of the Later Middle Ages.* Philadelphia: University of Pennsylvania Press, 2008.

Van Os, Henk. *The Art of Devotion in the Late Middle Ages in Europe, 1300-1500.* Princeton: Princeton University Press, 1994.

Voigt, Georg. *Die Wiederbelebung des classischen Alterthums.* 2 vols. 2d edn. Berlin: Verlag G. Reimer, 1880-1881.

Von Balthasar, Hans Urs. *Christian Meditation,* trans. Sister Mary Theresilde Skerry. San Francisco: Ignatius Press, 1989.

Von Balthasar, Hans Urs. *Elucidations,* trans. John Riches. San Francisco: Ignatius Press, 1998.

Waley, Daniel and Peter Denley. *Later Medieval Europe, 1250-1520.* 3d edn. Harlow: Longman, 2001.

Wallace, Robert M. "Progress, Secularization and Modernity: The Löwith-Blumenberg Debate." *New German Critique* 22 (1981): 63–79.

Walser, Ernst. *Gesammelte Studien zur Geistesgeschichte der Renaissance.* Basel: Verlag von Benno Schwabe & Co., 1932.

Walser, Ernst. *Studien zur Weltanschauung der Renaissance.* Basel: Benno Schwabe, 1920.

Weber, Max. "Science as a Vocation." In *The Vocation Lectures,* eds. David Owen and Tracy B. Strong, trans. Rodney Livingston, 1–31. New York: Hackett, 2004.

Wilson, Edmund. "A Preface to Persius: Maudlin Meditations in a Speakeasy." In Edmund Wilson, *The Shores of Light: A Literary Chronicle of the 1920s and 1930s,* 267–273. New York: Noonday Press, 1952.

Wind, Edgar. "Contemporary German Philosophy." *Journal of Philosophy* 22 (1925): 477–493, 516–530.

Wulf, Maurice de. *History of Mediaeval Philosophy,* trans. Ernest C. Messenger. 2 vols. London: Longmans, Green and Co., 1925-1926.

W. dreams, like Phaedrus, of an army of thinker-friends, thinker-lovers. He dreams of a thought-army, a thought-pack, which would storm the philosophical Houses of Parliament. He dreams of Tartars from the philosophical steppes, of thought-barbarians, thought-outsiders. What distances would shine in their eyes!

~Lars Iyer

www.babelworkinggroup.org

Michael Edward Moore is the author of *A Sacred Kingdom: Bishops and the Rise of Frankish Kingship, 300-850* (Catholic University of America Press, 2011), and of numerous essays on medieval and modern cultural and intellectual history. He has been a Visiting Research Fellow at Trinity College, an Andrew W. Mellon Fellow at the Library of Congress, and is currently Associate Professor in the Department of History, University of Iowa.

Made in the USA
Lexington, KY
11 May 2014